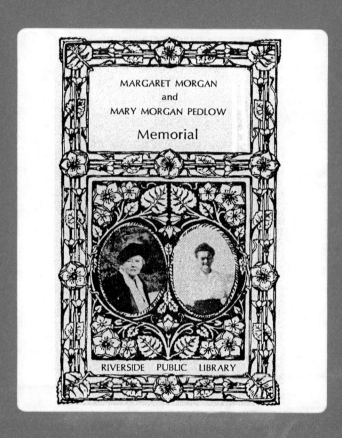

COLLECTING
STOCK CAR RACING
MEMORABILIA

THOMAS S. OWENS

The Millbrook Press   Brookfield, Connecticut

To Diana Star Helmer, my crew chief

The author wishes to thank the following people for their assistance and cooperation in providing illustrative materials for the interior and cover of this book: Greg Granillo, Elizabeth Turner, Steven Cole (Action Performance Companies, Inc.); Dave Phillips (www.raceimage.com); Justin Kanoya, Mary Mancera (The Upper Deck Company, LLC); Eddy Hickman (TeamCaliber); Tom Long (Georgia Marketing/Peachstate); Larry Blackwell, Michelle Duphorne (Playoff Corporation); Miles Atkins (Racing Champions); Clay Luraschi (Fleer Trading Cards); Dianne McClure (Racing Collectors Price Guide); Leslie Himley, Greg Zimprich (General Mills); Jack Cathey (www.raceshops.com)

Action Performance Companies, Inc.'s die-cast collectibles are available through the Racing Collectibles Club of America (RCCA), online at goracing.com, trackside at racing events, mass retail department stores, and a worldwide network of wholesale distributors and specialty dealers. To join RCCA, call 1-800-952-0708 or visit goracing.com. The nearest Action distributor can be found by calling 1-800-411-8404.

We acknowledge that some words, brand names and titles mentioned in this book are the property of the trademark holders. We use such terms for identification purposes only. This book is not a NASCAR®-sanctioned title.

Library of Congress Cataloging-in-Publication Data

Owens, Tom, 1960-
Collecting stock car racing memorabilia / Thomas S. Owens.
p. cm.
Includes bibliographical references and index.
ISBN 0-7613-1853-4 (lib. bdg.)
1. Stock car racing—Collectibles—United States—Juvenile literature. 2. NASCAR (Association)—Collectibles—Juvenile literature. [1. Stock car racing—Collectibles.] I. Title.

GV1029.9.S74 O92 2001
796.72'0973'075—dc21
00-048209

Published by The Millbrook Press, Inc.
2 Old New Milford Road
Brookfield, Connecticut 06804
www.millbrookpress.com

CONTENTS

1

SHRUNKEN CARS AND MORE!

From driver action figures to scrap rubber and metal from wrecks at the track, collectors of stock car racing memorabilia can—and do—save just about everything associated with NASCAR. But just as each lap of a race has leaders, stock car racing memorabilia has its leaders, too. In the hobby race, model cars and trading cards are the most popular contenders.

Die-Cast Cars

These small, replica cars have a strange-sounding name with a simple explanation. The metal bodies of such cars are made from a mold, or cast from a die. Molten metal is poured into molds. After it cools and hardens, the model is removed, cleaned, and painted. In many ways, the process is similar to making plaster-of-paris models. Nearly all die-cast manufacturing happens in countries outside of America, the home of stock car racing.

The description of a die-cast car always lists the driver's name and the sponsor or customized paint job, and then ends with numbers indicating the size of the model. If a 1:64 scale is listed, the die-cast is a shrunken image of that same NASCAR car, reduced to 1/64th the size of the original car. A full-size car would be 1:1. Familiar to collectors of Hot Wheels or Matchbox cars, 1:64 cars are approximately 3 inches (7.5 cm) long.

Having *the* car for a driver isn't the way in today's die-cast market. Cars may have a special paint scheme for only one race.

DALE EARNHARDT WON HIS 75TH CAREER NASCAR WINSTON CUP RACE AT ATLANTA MOTOR SPEEDWAY IN MARCH, 2000. TO HONOR HIS MILESTONE, ACTION PRODUCED A PLATINUM-PLATED VERSION OF HIS WINNING NO. 3 CHEVROLET MONTE CARLO. (IMAGE COURTESY OF ACTION PERFORMANCE COMPANIES, INC. USED WITH PERMISSION.)

THIS REPLICA DEPICTS DALE JARRETT'S CAR FROM HIS FIRST CHAMPIONSHIP IN 1999. (IMAGE COURTESY OF ACTION PERFORMANCE COMPANIES, INC. USED WITH PERMISSION.)

DURING THE 1999 HOMESTEAD-MIAMI NASCAR RACE, JEFF GORDON'S AND BOBBY LABONTE'S CARS FEATURED SPECIAL NASCAR RACERS PAINT SCHEMES DESIGNED BY ACTION PERFORMANCE. (IMAGE COURTESY OF ACTION PERFORMANCE COMPANIES, INC. USED WITH PERMISSION.)

The cars sometimes seem like metal billboards, zooming with new messages every week. Die-cast companies hope you'll buy every variety of car driven by your favorite driver. Is your Jeff Gordon the Jurassic Park version, the Peanuts version, the Dupont car, or the Dupont "Chromalusion" variety? New seasons bring new die-cast choices.

Another way to arrange your collection is to show your driver's car growing—or shrinking. Popular sizes of die-cast replicas include 1:18, 1:24, 1:43, 1:64, and 1:144, which is about 1 inch (2.5 cm) long. Die-cast fever has even spread to transporters (the trucks that haul the cars), pit wagons (toolboxes on wheels that are hauled from the garage to pit row), and cars made into banks.

The suggested retail values of the biggest scaled-down cars (1:18) can run anywhere from twenty dollars to hundreds of dollars. The biggest versions allow for the most details, making a 1:24 almost a small statue of the car.

Differences in the products may include sponsor decals versus stickers (decals are harder to remove); rubber or plastic tires; trunks and hoods, which may or may not open; and fixed bodies versus car bodies that can be removed from the chassis (frame).

Die-Cast, Not For Kids?

Stickers, wheels, moving parts—these cars sound like toys. But are they? Some die-cast cars have the words "adult collectible" stamped on the package. Why wouldn't companies want kids to play with their toys?

PEACHSTATE PRODUCED 1:64 SCALE DIE-CAST TRANSPORTERS OF THE MARK MARTIN AND VALVOLINE RACING TEAM IN 1997, TODD BODINE AND TEAM TABASCO IN 1998, AND TONY STEWART'S JOE GIBBS RACING ENTRY IN 2000. ALL DIE-CAST WERE SERIAL NUMBERED IN LIMITED EDITIONS: MARTIN (2,004), BODINE (1,144), AND STEWART (2,400). (IMAGES COURTESY OF GEORGIA MARKETING/PEACHSTATE)

The confusion may have started with Matchbox or Hot Wheels. These two toy-makers started making die-cast cars decades ago, combining them with track and other ways to play. But when the companies began producing NASCAR replicas—Matchbox in 1990 and Hot Wheels in 1997—the world suddenly wondered if cars with alcohol and tobacco connections should be sold to kids. Did cigarette logos send the wrong message?

The company Action Racing Collectibles tried to discourage young people from buying their replicas by making the cars difficult to play with. They mounted "controversial" cars on a base and sometimes packaged them in acrylic cases.

But die-cast companies didn't need to worry. The 1:64 scale cars that are so common in toy departments of major stores usually remain wrapped. Die-cast collectors young and old know that collectibles lose half their value if taken out of the package. As a result, the "blister packs" that are used to hang the die-cast packages on store racks stay in place, even when companies include cards or other bonuses. Opening the pack to enjoy the extra collectible would be a value-busting move—and kids of all ages know it.

The federal government didn't agree. The government decided that teams such as Jimmy Spencer's 1997 "Smokin' Joe's" team, which featured the controversial Camel Cigarettes cartoon mascot, encouraged kids to smoke. Tobacco companies finally promised not to use their logos on die-cast cars beginning June 30, 1999.

Cards

The J.R. Maxx company ushered in the modern era of NASCAR cards in 1988. Collectors finally had collectible cards of drivers, tracks, and pit-crew members. The design of these cards seems plain by today's standards.

The Maxx company went out of business in 1996. That year, there was a huge increase in NASCAR card production—nine different companies were competing. Upper Deck took over Maxx and began issuing new sets under the old name in 1997, while continuing with its own name on some other sets. Upper Deck's PowerDeck insert cards featured a CD-ROM that included a multimedia biography of the driver.

For its 1993 debut, the company Action Packed introduced a raised, three-dimensional surface to racing cards. The price of $2.99 for six cards was double the

price charged by other companies. But the imaginative designs of Action Packed were unmatched. The company even applied its paper-sculpting technology to create cards in Braille for blind fans.

The company Press Pass was also created in 1993. This was the first company to issue its set of cards before the NASCAR season started. In 1996, Press Pass included race-used inserts in its "Burning Rubber" cards. Press Pass was the first company to introduce a piece of a tire from the pictured car within the card set. The company later included sheet metal, fire suits, and other race artifacts.

Three Sets Remain

Other companies found it easier to compete in the battle of random autographs, promising specially signed cards in select packs. But as the 1990s ended, few companies remained. The only brand names to enter the year 2000 were Upper Deck, Press Pass, and High Gear. Companies were making fewer cards, while more fanciful inserts were being offered to spice up the attraction of opening packs.

Cars and cards are still the main collectibles, but the hobby is far from a two-category race. Autographs, hero cards/postcards, model kits, action figures, programs, ticket stubs, and a lot more battle for a place in the hearts of collectors. As old companies fade away and new producers appear, each season creates a new race for hobbyist dollars.

Drivers, start your engines!

Collectors, start your hobby!

CONDITION: WHEN CARDS GO BAD

By lap 400 of the Daytona 500, surviving cars might look like ugly imitators of the shiny starters. Racing cards meet up with assorted scrapes, too. And when it comes to determining how much money a card is worth, condition matters more than the name and face on the front of the card. A Jeff Gordon card in poor condition shouldn't bring any more money, or interest, than a shredded card of any no-name journeyman driver.

Collectors grade all cards on the same scale—no matter how new or old the cards are, no matter how famous the faces. Card conditions with their common abbreviations include:

Mint (MT)

A mint card has no problems, large or small. In fact, the word "mint" means new, or just made. A mint card has four sharp corners, a well-centered picture with borders equal on all sides, and all edges intact. The card still has a shine, with no scratches from handling and no fading from too much light. Likewise, a mint card is free from all printing problems, such as ink blobs or out-of-focus images.

To some hobby minds, "mint" means in perfect, *original* condition. Cards printed in sheets or on cereal boxes should not be cut out if you want the cards to be considered mint.

Near Mint (NRMT)

In school terms, this is an "A–" instead of an "A+." This card has one minor flaw, easier to spot. To fall to NRMT status, a card might have one corner that has lost most of its point, or all the corners might have a small amount of wear. The image on the card front may be slightly off-center for one border. Printing quality may be less than perfect. One or both card sides might have been very slightly scraped. However, the card surfaces are still bright, shiny, and smooth.

Excellent (EX)

This uncreased card has corners that are mostly sharp but not perfect. Off-center borders may appear, along with a slight scuff or dullness from rubbing against other cards.

Very Good (VG)

Sharp corners disappear from VG cards. Minor creases (folds or tears in the card) followed by gum stains or package damage are common problems. However, there are no tape damages, huge creases, or ink damages.

Good (G), Fair (F), Poor (P)

The grades start getting scarier here. G, F, and P hobby grades might match a "C−," "D," and "F" in school. The grade depends on how injured the card looks. These cards have different degrees of major damage. Large and small creases may be found, and all four corners may have varying kinds of wear. Card fronts are scuffed, with little gloss remaining.

In 1997, Pinnacle Precision's 77-card set was all steel. Four cards came in a metal container shaped like an oil can, with a suggested retail price of $9.99. Collectors puzzled over whether to peel the protective film off the cards, like this one of owner Roger Penske (left). The company stressed that the cards would have a better condition, but collectors hated not seeing the photo. (Courtesy of Playoff Corporation)

Tough Calls

Some card problems are easy to spot. But others are trickier—the difference between an "A+" and an "A." Card injuries often begin on the corners. At one time, all four corners were sharp and straight, precise right angles. Are they still? Card graders give corners five different grades, similar to "A" through "F" school grades, to note a corner's five stages of wear. Worn corners can make a card become more circular than its original rectangular shape.

Alignment is another common woe. Most older card photos were framed by four borders. Cards sometimes lack part of one or two borders, with the photograph appearing to fall off the front of the card. This often happens during manufacturing, when machines cut sheets of 110 to 132 cards (depending on set size).

Some dealers might brag that cards are "straight out of the pack" or "from a factory-collated set." The message is that cards never touched by hobbyists' hands are in better shape. But machines make mistakes, too. Collectors sometimes find miscuts with half of two different cards sharing one card front!

But many older cards simply suffer from time, from incorrect storage, or from too much love. The worst creases interrupt the photo on the card front, or destroy part of the cardboard.

Hobbyists buying older cards need to be careful. Condition determines cost, and sellers have ways to hide card problems—then charge more money.

Suppose a black-bordered card has a chip or ding. A wrongdoer could cover the mark with crayon or marker. A tougher trick to catch is the trimmed card. If a border is

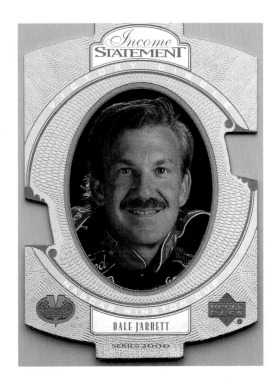

THE "INCOME STATEMENT" INSERTS FROM PACKS OF 2000 UPPER DECK VICTORY CIRCLE WERE PRETTY EASY TO COME BY. WRAPPERS STATED ODDS THAT 1 OF EVERY 9 PACKS MIGHT HAVE THE INSERT. (COURTESY OF UPPER DECK, LLC)

uneven or worn, the card is shaved with a paper cutter to make it appear straight and mint again. Only by using another card from that same set is it possible to discover that the altered card may be slightly smaller.

Whose Cards Are Best?

What if a wounded card isn't retouched? Is a card in fair-to-good condition worth the bother at all? Many dealers would tell you that a card in poor condition is worth only 20 percent of the amount the same card in mint condition would bring. But many collectors would say the card is a worthwhile "filler." If you are trying to complete a set—for instance, one of every Bobby Labonte card that you can find—a filler card will bring you closer to your goal. After you finish your set, you can always look for nicer versions of certain cards.

As the twenty-first century began, grading services competed to make card conditions official. Collectors would pay anywhere from $5 to $50 to send a card to a grader. The card would be returned in a sealed, protective holder, or slab. A label attached would verify that the card wasn't counterfeit, and would describe the condition of the card upon sealing. Coin collectors had adopted this practice years before.

The problem? Every service would choose a different scale, either 1 to 10 or 1 to 100. Confusion grew over which grading company knew best. Nevertheless, some collectors began paying ten to twenty times the price-guide rates for cards with the best grades.

IN 1999, DALE EARNHARDT AUTOGRAPHED JUST 700 RANDOMLY INSERTED CARDS FOR PRESS PASS. THE COMPANY PIONEERED THE CONCEPT OF MAKING CARDS OUT OF RACE-USED MATERIAL, SUCH AS CHUNKS OF TIRES OR SWATCHES OF FIRESUITS. (COURTESY OF RACING CHAMPIONS INC.)

Keep in mind that beauty is in the eye of the beholder. Your dog may be the ugliest dog in the world, but you believe no dog is better. Likewise, in the sports-card hobby, condition is in the eye of the beholder.

Would you be surprised to learn that many sellers overgrade their cards? That means, "My card is great, so pay me a lot." Of course, buyers want to undergrade, meaning, "I want that card cheaper." Before buying, it's best to see a card in person, up-close, to know its true condition. To get the best viewing of a card, examine the card in good light and out of its protective holder, if possible.

A card's condition determines its cost. This matters most when you are buying. So decide why you are buying the card in the first place.

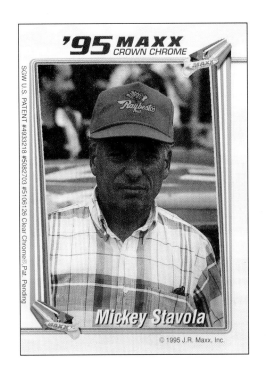

A BACKLESS CARD? THE 1995 MAXX CROWN CHROME IS A CLEAR PLASTIC PARALLEL TO THE 185-CARD PREMIER PLUS SET. (COURTESY OF UPPER DECK COMPANY, LLC)

Dealers will tell you that only mint cards are "collectible." But in hobby-speak, collectible means "worth money." If you want any card of a rising star like Jason Jarrett because your collection is of the Jarrett family, consider paying less for a lesser-condition card. Worry about great condition only if you plan to sell the card later.

Remember, *collectible* and *condition* are somebody else's rules. If your collection is just for you, you can make the rules. You can measure your success any way you want. Money is one measure of success. But fun and pride are important considerations, too.

CYBER-COLLECTING

New cars. New cards. Buying. Selling. Trading.

Where? At your crosstown hobby shop, or the annual card show?

Try a computer!

With fast, nonstop hobby action, computers are changing how collectors collect. With the Internet, you don't have to wait for hobby magazines to get the news, print it, and mail it. Just log onto the team sponsor's Web site. Under "news releases" are the same stories about new sets that are sent to hobby magazines. In fact, you might see almost the same story printed in the hobby magazines several weeks later. News doesn't play favorites online. Everyone with a computer, at home, at school, or in the library, can get information at the same time.

Early information can help collectors budget their hobby dollars. For example, in the summer of 2000, Upper Deck's Web site tipped off collectors that the company was ready to launch a role-playing game featuring NASCAR stars. Interested hobbyists knew to hold off on buying another card set until they had a chance to see the new product.

But one of the most exciting ways the Internet helps increase your collection is with access to race teams. The Internet can show you which tracks or team sponsors are the hobby-friendliest. You can check out upcoming schedules and races online. Those schedules may list promotional giveaways, giving you an idea of which speedways reward their fans with free cards, autograph signings, or other treats.

Collecting Questions

Even if the information you're looking for isn't listed, you can ask for it. The Internet is an equal-opportunity medium. Your message, sent by electronic (e-) mail, often gets instant attention. As long as your spelling and grammar are all-star quality, there is no clue that you're a kid. You're judged by your message or your request.

True, some companies are slow to provide a space for feedback. Their Web sites are advertisements only. But other sponsors reach out to fans by hosting online chats—opportunities to ask questions of a driver or team member by typing them messages. Their response will come in real time. For example, if Joe Gearshift is scheduled for a one-hour chat, you'll know if your question will or won't be answered in that time slot. Other racing Web sites give you more time. Web visitors are given a chance to post questions to a specified team member, who will post replies the following week in the same section.

Sweepstakes and online contests are Internet bonuses used by still other corporate sponsors of race teams, such as Coca-Cola. Be sure to get permission from an adult before registering online for contests or free newsletters, or any time when your personal information is requested.

Don't stop with the Web sites of big-business sponsors. Race teams and drivers have found that the Internet is a fast and easy way to communicate with their countless fans, too. Team Web sites should have instructions about:

- if and when tours of the team shop are available
- how autograph requests should be sent
- how fans can join a fan club
- if special collectibles are sold to Internet visitors
- where the driver or show car will appear

Sometimes special prices, or even a special souvenir, might be offered only through the official Web site.

Collecting Craven

During the 2000 season, driver Ricky Craven sold autographed cards of himself from past sets, often for as little as $2.50 each. His Web site pictured all the cards, with the illustrations creating a mini hobby museum. Other drivers and teams have

held Internet auctions, offering sheet metal from wrecked cars or other race-used memorabilia. The proceeds usually go to a favorite charity.

Fans often create great Web sites of their favorite drivers, too. These volunteer Web masters simply adore the driver they honor. Many fan-created Web sites have "guest books." Write a note online saying how you like the site. It's a great chance to get questions answered about that driver, or to meet other hobbyists.

Hobbyists can learn a lot online, swapping information and more. Shops, dealers, and individual collectors can contact each other through forums, bulletin boards, chat rooms, or personally created Web sites. They can leave messages about the memorabilia they have or want, offering to buy, sell, or trade. One of the most popular free Web sites for hobbyists is www.beckett.com, created by the famed hobby magazine.

From such a site, registered members have "profiles." Here, it's possible to leave feedback about someone you've dealt with—or check out someone you're considering doing business with. Visitors may find subject lines like "Bad Trader" or "Ripped off." A common story found under such headings tells of two online collectors who agreed to trade one card each. The first collector was honest and sent his trade through the mail. But the second trader claimed the card never arrived and wouldn't send the card he promised in return. Many such stories involve inserts or rookie cards, with losses in the tens and hundreds of dollars.

Horrible Hobbyists?

How do you know who is telling the truth, the accuser or the accused? After all, the remote chance exists for someone to play a prank and falsely charge another.

For the most part, people share sad stories because they're trying to help others avoid the problems they found. But in the long run, being more choosy about hobby partners will help traders escape such disappointments.

If you spend a couple of dollars extra to send your trade by registered mail or United Parcel Service, you'll get a receipt after your package is delivered—written proof that it reached its destination. If you have such information, your postmaster or the Better Business Bureau (check your local telephone directory) might be able to help you get the goods that were promised in trade. But, most often, the best defense is a good offense. In other words, check out the person you're dealing with before you send money or trades.

Collectors of any age should talk by telephone or mail a regular letter

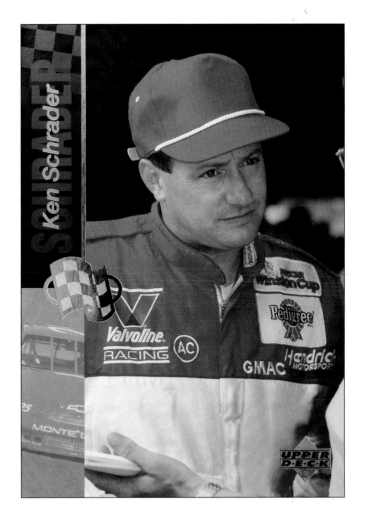

My, how cards grow! In 1995, Upper Deck offered a 5-by-7-inch oversized version of 10 different cards, one per box of foil packs. (Courtesy of Upper Deck, LLC)

to get more information from new hobby people they meet on the Internet. It's a good idea to ask for names of people that your new trading partner has done business with. Then call or write those people, too. Dealers who won't give you names of other people they've done hobby business with aren't worth your time. It's your money and your memorabilia.

Don't be shy about asking for opinions from teachers or other adults who've done business on the Internet before. They can help you judge if the sales pitches or trade offers sound fair and honest. We all need to be reminded sometimes of the old, wise warning: "If something sounds too good to be true, it probably is."

Auction Action

On the Beckett Web site, collector auctions happen daily. But the most famous auction Web site at the start of the twenty-first century was www.ebay.com. On weekends, when traffic was highest on the Web site, ebay often hosted at least 20,000 different NASCAR lots. A lot is either a single item or a combination of items. A rising star in the hobby field was www.sportsauction.com.

FLEER ULTRA ISSUED 97 EXTRA CARDS IN 1997, CALLING ITS SECOND OFFERING AN "UPDATE" SET. (COURTESY OF FLEER TRADING CARDS)

FLEER'S 1996 "FLAIR" SET OF 100 CARDS FEATURED ETCHED FOIL, WITH DOUBLE THE THICKNESS OF MANY CARDS. A FIVE-CARD PACK'S SUGGESTED RETAIL WAS $4.99. (COURTESY OF FLEER TRADING CARDS)

The bad news? No one under the age of eighteen was eligible to bid on these sites. Minors who wanted to bid were required to have an adult bid for them. Why? Pretending to bid on an item, then not paying for it, is more than wrong. It's against the law in many states. A bidder's word is a legal contract. Bidders who don't honor their bids might face lawsuits.

But younger collectors can still use these sites as yardsticks to measure hobby activity. Are actual selling prices above or below price-guide listings? Best of all, almost all cards sold by Internet auction are shown online. Auction Web sites are like museums. You can look and learn for free, without buying anything!

Hobbyists can learn more about basic collecting online, too. Sometimes bulletin boards or forums give a chance for visitors to post a comment or question for the world to consider. See if others will share their collecting experiences, such as: Did they fail to get a complete set after opening a box of packs? Did they get more inserts than the odds on the wrapper predicted? By sharing information, all collectors can spend their money more wisely and get the cards they want most.

Many public schools in many states have their own Web sites. Find a student race fan who wants an "e" pen pal, and there's a chance you'll find a collector who would trade cards.

Any time the e-mail address of a race team, hobby author, cardmaker, or dealer is printed in an article or on a package, keep track of it. That hints that the person or company wants to know what you're thinking. Send your questions and ideas. Don't think: "Why would someone answer me?" Instead, try asking: "Why not?"

Sorting Out Sponsors

Countless NASCAR fans have imagined the unknown hero before: The fan who gets a job around the team shop. The job leads to a *ride* as a team driver. Then the driver becomes a champion.

If you want to see the top "rags to riches" stories of stock-car fandom, visit www.jayski.com. Race-team representatives say it. Reporters do, too. This is the place with the best free news about who's racing for whom.

Why do collectors need to keep informed about sponsors? If a company drops a team, the stream of collectibles dries up. Likewise, if a new team owner hires

KYLE PETTY AND HIS CREW MEMBERS WORE SPECIAL FIRE-SUITS FOR PART OF THE 1999 SEASON IN ANTICIPATION OF THE NEW DISNEY MOVIE. (COURTESY OF DAVE PHILLIPS)

away a driver, there are bound to be surprise issues of postcards and other memorabilia updating the partnership before the season ends. In fact, the end of the season traditionally results in so much sponsor-swapping that fans call it "Silly Season." That's the name of the Web site, too.

In early 2000, the company Racing Champions Ertl became official sponsor of www.jayski.com. Those advertising dollars guaranteed that the seldom-seen Web master could keep uncovering the truth behind those sponsor-switching, driver-shuffling rumors. And die-cast fans could keep flocking to see "DieCast Express," free classified ads for all collectors.

Who is "Jay," the brains behind the acclaimed racing Web site that advocates news and destroys rumors? Jay Adamczyk doesn't post his full name or photo anywhere. Like a comic-book hero, he keeps his identity secret. In past Web postings, he revealed only tidbits about his history as a NASCAR detective.

"Back in August of 1996, I heard that Lake Speed was losing the Spam sponsorship and would be sponsored by the University of Nebraska. I searched and searched and could not find a thing about it on the Internet," Jay said. "So I started posting things to the r.a.s.n. (Rec.Autos.Sport.NASCAR) newsgroup. The posts kept growing and were getting too difficult to continue everyday. So I decided to make a little page about the Silly Season news."

"I remember when I had 100 visitors in one day, I thought that was amazing. The page now [gets] over 50,000 a day," he said. By the year 2000, Jay worked sometimes more than 100 hours weekly, maintaining the site's 400-plus pages.

SHOWS: A COLLECTION OF DEALERS

Racing collectibles dealers have collections of motorsports memorabilia. Racing collectibles shows are collections of racing dealers.

There they are, all under one roof, like a mall full of nothing but hobby shops. Dealers come together for a show, bringing some of their best items. They manage tables filled with various die-cast cars, racing cards, and collectibles.

If the first table you stop at doesn't have that Jeff Burton die-cast you want, move on. Or if that first dealer wants too much money for the die-cast, see if a seller down the line is willing to listen to offers.

That's right, sometimes you can make a deal. Although show dealers have to pay for their trip to the show, including food, gas, and maybe an overnight stay in a hotel, many dealers don't have other ongoing expenses. True, some card-show dealers have actual shops back home. But others just run mail-order businesses and come to hobby shows.

Are Real Dealers Best?

These "weekend warriors" are part-time dealers who have regular, nonhobby jobs. They deal memorabilia simply to earn money to build their own collections, not for food and clothes. A one-time rental fee for a space at the show is their main cost. And if dealers are spending less money on their businesses, they might not mind making less profit.

A hobby show is the best place to compare cards and prices. To get the most out of your visit, start by knowing the show. Big or small? For a smaller event, make sure to call one or two days beforehand. Think how sad it would be to travel an hour

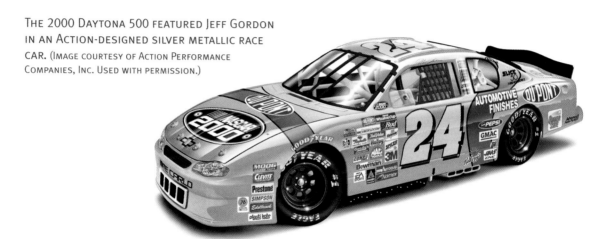

or more only to find that the event has been canceled. Bigger shows are less likely to be called off and more likely to offer lots of choice. But is bigger best? Not always.

"All-sports shows" may be much heavier into baseball, basketball, and football memorabilia than racing. You may find only two dealers with NASCAR items at a 50-table show—and chances are that prices will be the same between sellers.

Yet this could work to your advantage. Dealers who specialize in other sports may come to an all-sports show with hopes of dumping unwanted NASCAR items—sometimes at huge discounts. But all things considered, most racing collectors prefer racing shows, where selection from *their* sport is biggest.

Racing Show Freebies

When you are reading advertisements for larger, regional shows, look at the fine print. Along with admission fees, information about corporate sponsors or partners might be listed. If you see the logos for Upper Deck, Racing Champions, or other manufacturers in an advertisement, get excited. Often, companies will set up booths at bigger shows. They will hold contests, have employees answer questions about new collectibles, and even give away the promotional samples collectors crave.

But no matter what size show you want to attend, get your game plan set. Here are some helpful shopping strategies:

Race in the Off-Season

Racing dealers in Kentucky sometimes have their own special pricing system. Collectibles featuring Jeremy Mayfield or Darrell Waltrip might cost a little more in that state than any price-guide quotes.

What did those racers do to go up in value? They were born in Kentucky. Even if someone from California enjoyed his first racing successes on small tracks in Kentucky, fans and dealers in Kentucky will remember. Remember now where drivers get their starts, and you might be able to profit later.

Likewise, shopping at the *wrong* times might offer the *right* prices.

A one-sided NASCAR season might be the best opening a collector can imagine. Drivers who are out of the race for the points championship may have switched teams or sponsors. While many fans hold out for current die-casts to be made, smart collectors might find older items at discount prices.

The Middle Comes Last

Hobby history shows that the best prices and deals come in the opening, or closing, hours of an event.

Dealers often have two mind-sets. Some may want to make as much money as fast as possible to ensure they make back table rental and travel expenses. Other dealers might be stingy until the final moments of the show. Then, realizing that sales figures were disappointing, they'll choose to give you a deal. That way, they'll have some money to show for their work—and have a lighter load to carry home.

Feel the Deal

Asking a dealer to sell an item for less money might seem harder than passing an Earnhardt on the race's last lap. Just remember, anything's possible—but some ground rules can help your odds!

• It's best to go one-on-one with a dealer.

Time your drive. Asking the dealer to sell you a two-dollar card for a buck in the middle of a crowd of collectors can bring doom. Most dealers will say no, knowing that everyone else listening will crow, "Hey! Sell to me at half-price, too!"

• Discounts may be as easy as one-two-three.

A three-step negotiation can work. Imagine this matchup:

> *Dealer:* That Jason Keller card books at three bucks.
> *Kid Collector:* How about a dollar?
> *Dealer:* I need at least two dollars.
> *Kid Collector:* Sold!

COLLECTOR SHOWS PROVE HOW IMPORTANT THE EVERYDAY SPONSORS AND ADVERTISERS ARE TO NASCAR. ONE NOTED OUTDOOR SHOW IS HELD YEARLY OUTSIDE LOWE'S MOTOR SPEEDWAY IN CHARLOTTE, NORTH CAROLINA. SHOWS LIKE THESE INVOLVE TRACKSIDE TRAILERS, THE SAME SOUVENIR SHOPS-ON-WHEELS THAT TRAVEL FROM RACE TO RACE. (COURTESY OF RACING COLLECTOR'S PRICE GUIDE, WWW.RACINGCOLLECTORS.COM)

Do the math. See how the card was priced three times, and the price changed by one-third? A price reduction of 25 percent (taking a quarter off for every dollar) is common. A 33 percent reduction (of $3 to $2) is possible. A half-price discount is a rare win.

Note that most dealers will laugh (or swear!) and stomp away when someone asks for more than half off a card. For instance, if a price guide claims that the new John Andretti die-cast should sell for $10, you might make your case with a $5 offer. Offer only $2, and you'll probably get a nasty response from the other side of the table. A common dealer response to such low-ball offers sounds something like this: "If you think my stuff is so worthless, why are you wasting your time and mine?"

Furthermore, don't try to fib, saying, "The dealer over there sells it cheaper." The likely dealer reply will be, "Fine. Go buy it there." Dealers scout their competition. They know their prices have to be at or below other prices in the room. Worse yet, collectors who try to make dealers oppose each other for lowest prices may get shunned by every seller. Believe it or not, many dealers are friends who stick together.

Bring Reading Material

Do you have a recent price-guide magazine? Be sure to bring it to the next show you attend. It's like having another person beside you to help negotiate your purchase.

These days, most dealers won't bother putting prices on many single cards. Instead, they'll flip open their *Beckett* and tell you how much the magazine guesses those cards or die-casts are worth. Still, have a magazine of your own. If a dealer is sure the card you want should cost $5, instead of the dollar that the price guide claims, politely point out the difference. It's fine to say, "I was hoping to get the card for book value." Some dealers might agree to meet the price. Others may explain why they want more. Maybe they paid the *Beckett* price, expecting the card to become a hot property in the future. Even if you decide not to buy the card, you'll still get a free education about future hobby trends.

Choose Your Groove

The nice thing about a hobby show is that only you decide which dealers get your business. That's why, at a show crammed with tables, you'll want to pick your sellers carefully.

When you have money to spend, you're in the lead. You don't have to waste time at a huge show with a dealer who doesn't mark prices on any items. Some tables may have tons of cards, all without a single price. These dealers may be slowpokes who want to study their price guides, taking forever to decide how much to ask for each card.

Other dealers want to play a guessing game. They look at you, trying to guess how much you'd be willing to pay, even saying, "Make me an offer." This could be a clue that the dealer is wondering how much he can overcharge an unknowing hobbyist.

Go first to dealers who put prices on their collectibles. They are being honest, telling everyone how much money they want with the price tags they use. Then, with one look, you can decide if the deal is for you.

Bag It

You may not get the best service at a show. With dozens of customers anxious to buy now, the dealer may not even offer you a protective holder for your new Mark Martin card. Or, after you've purchased fifty different Press Pass cards, you might wonder how you'll carry all your purchases around the room or all the way home. Many dealers don't think to bring bags for their customers.

It's not fun to spend your remaining shopping dollars on cardholders. However, bending new cards to fit in your pocket doesn't make sense, either. The answer? Carry a backpack, a book bag, or some other way to tote your buys, and bring some kind of empty card protectors.

Almost every dealer has seen a customer running around a hobby show asking for help finding a lost card. The collector bought a card, carried it by hand, and then laid it down while browsing at another table. Of course, the proud purchase often disappears. Don't let it happen to you.

Watch the Order

Many dealers seem to see nothing wrong with giving you unbagged, unprotected cards, endangering the mint conditions. But dealers have some gripes about young customers, too.

Dealers often catch collectors pulling commons, or unpopular cards, that were once in numerical order out of huge piles. Suddenly, the young hobbyist doesn't want to buy all those cards. Not only does the dealer make no money, but he has to ignore other customers while resorting and

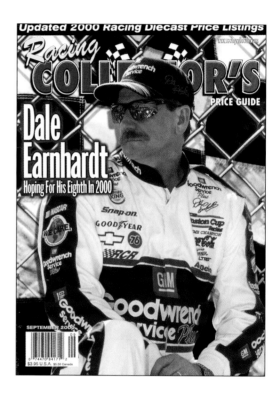

refiling the unwanted cards back in numerical order. That's why some dealers stop carrying commons—they take too much time and make too little money.

Here's an easy solution for the collector and the dealer. Bring a handful of 3-by-5-inch (7.6-by-12.7-cm) index cards with you when you shop. Before you look over commons, show the dealer that you'll mark the places of the cards you pull for consideration. You can say, "I'll keep them in order by number this way. Okay?" Watch the dealer's face shine. Maybe your thoughtfulness will even get you a better deal for less money.

Skip the Trades

A hobby show isn't an easy place for you to swap with a dealer. Even a fair, friendly dealer has to think about earning a living. The shopping mall or hotel usually charges table rental space, and the gas, food, and hotel bills before and after the show won't be small. Remember the old saying, "Time is money." That's why many dealers would rather spend five minutes selling to as many customers as possible, instead of working out one moneyless deal with you—which you might turn down at the last minute.

Dealers get squeezed at every show. What inventory can fit on one table—a space often 4 by 12 feet (1.2 by 3.6 meters), sometimes smaller? A collection of larger items, such as cereal boxes, might eat up all a dealer's showroom.

That's why some dealers might have the best and cheapest stuff hidden under the table. Unless you ask the right questions, you may never see them. Be patient, and specific, when you're shopping at shows.

Don't Miss the List

Any smart adult headed to buy groceries makes a list first. At the store, it's easy to forget the milk when surrounded by so many choices, or come home with nothing but potato chips and other fun food.

Surprisingly, few collectors bring a list of their wants to a hobby show. Some shoppers might insist that they know what they need or like without writing it down. Others think that the fun of a hobby show is buying the first new cards they see.

These mind-sets cause a few problems. Suppose the box of Upper Deck packs you opened left you short of a set by just seven cards. Unless you memorize the card numbers you need, you might blow your chance to complete the run of cards for a low price.

Also, don't get fooled by a big "sale" sign or fancy table display. Don't bite—or buy!—when a dealer says, "That's my last one. They're selling fast." Was the card on your list to begin with? Are you being competitive, trying to buy something just so other collectors won't get it?

Most important, your list helps you make a budget. Use hobby magazines and price guides to estimate the going rates for the cards you want. Write down the amount that you are willing and able to spend for each item. Having it in writing will help you to tell a dealer, "I wanted that High Gear set, but can't pay more than twelve dollars for it." These steps will help increase your chances of leaving the show with the cards you need and, maybe, a few bucks to spare.

Talk to Strangers

Dealers aren't the only people you should speak with at a show. Other customers can offer time-saving and money-saving tips. If you're at a show that has fifty dealer tables, shopping the whole area for the best price on a new Hot Wheels might take all day. So, if you see someone peeking under a 1:64 hood in the hotel lobby outside the showroom, ask for advice. "Excuse me, please. Do you remember which dealer you bought that from? Could I ask how much it cost?" Sometimes, such chats lead to free trading among show attendees. Best of all, you could make a friendship that might last beyond the day's event.

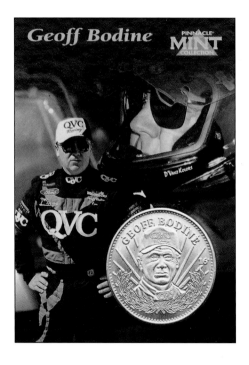 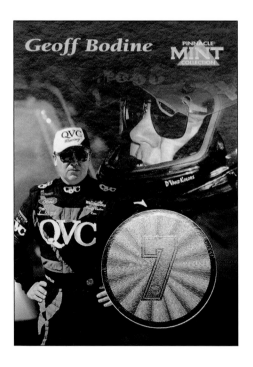

PINNACLE'S 1997 "MINT" SET COMBINED THE FUN OF TWO HOBBIES: CARDS AND COINS. ONE $2.99 PACK INCLUDED TWO DIE-CUT CARDS, TWO COINS, AND A REGULAR CARD. THE NUMBER OF THE CARD IS THE DRIVER'S CAR NUMBER. (COURTESY OF PLAYOFF CORPORATION)

AVOIDING HOBBY CRASHES

A good driver knows the secrets of the speedway. A good collector knows the curves of the hobby, including times to pass or slow down.

Drivers like to avoid unplanned pit stops. Collectors want to escape hobby pitfalls. Here are some hobby myths that sidetrack even advanced collectors:

1. Buying early is best.

Imagine that the season-opening Daytona 500 race is less than a month away. Fans travel to the convention-like Winston Cup Preview. They hunt for autographs from the many drivers in attendance, and they feast their eyes on the cars' new paint schemes.

And look—die-casts of the just-unveiled car design are already on sale! It seems like a good idea to get one. After all, won't prices zoom as more people learn about the car? Maybe. Hobby magazines and Web sites announce which releases are newest and scarcest. The price of collectibles made in the smallest amounts are more likely to climb faster.

On the other hand, if Dealer X discovers that he's among the first hobby merchants to carry a new item, he may feel entitled to pump up his prices. Furthermore, what if the driver depicted finishes in the Bottom 10 of points standings for the year? Or if that driver and sponsor part ways after only a handful of races? Prices will have nowhere to go but down.

2. Biggest names make the best collectibles.

"Who's he? Oh, that guy," is a hobbyist's common response to a driver who's had little success. Meanwhile, the dealer hauls out tons of Jeff Gordon stuff. Who wouldn't know one of the winners? Or what about retired legends like Richard Petty? No one can argue with history.

Is bigger better? Pinnacle thought so, issuing a set of 8-by-10 photos in its 1997 "Portraits" set. (Courtesy of Playoff Corporation)

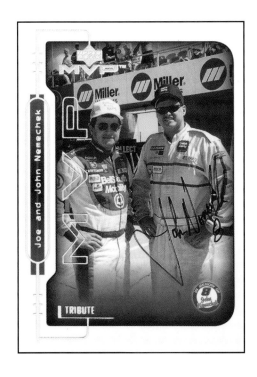

Not surprisingly, collecting only established winners is often more costly. Dealers may charge double the going rate for a current champion, explaining, "He's a star!" But this pricing philosophy may not apply to all stars. The hobby world often has a "What have you done lately?" attitude. It doesn't matter if the driver set records a year ago or twenty years ago (and those marks still stand). Household names like Jarrett or Gordon may show steady but tiny gains in price guides, or simply have values that hold stable for a year or two. Meanwhile, whoever won in the last month will get the most hobby applause.

3. Collect limited editions only.

This debate creates a huge speed-bump for many collectors. Sure, it makes sense that a "1 of 100" item will make you and the 99 other owners happy (or the 101st hobbyist ache with jealousy). Hobbyists often pay extra for these bragging rights.

But look carefully. The first pitfall is often the word *Limited*. How limited should limited be? In general, any edition over 10,000 items may not seem that hard to find. Would an edition of 10,000 provide one apiece to every person in your town? Be wary of any company wanting big bucks for a collectible that has *only* 25,000 made.

DON'T BE SCARED IF A COLLECTOR EVER TALKS ABOUT OWNING DALE JARRETT'S "NOSE." IT MEANS THE NOSE OF HIS CAR! (IMAGE COURTESY OF DAVE PHILLIPS)

Read the fine print. Some companies that make commemorative plates advertise "limited editions," boasting in smaller print that production was "limited to only 100 firing days." Translated, this means that the company made that kind of plate for 100 days. But were a million plates produced per day?

And remember: Limited editions don't have to cost a mint. Companies like Mattel are making hometown toy departments into limited-edition centers. Sometimes, the company will advertise that only one special edition die-cast or action figure will be included per box of product. Your odds might be 1 in 50 of finding the limited item. Maybe a different color or a certain driver gets the limited treatment. The stores put the special item out on the rack with all the regular products, selling it all at the same price. The only extra cost to the collector is in the time spent searching store shelves for the limited edition.

4. "That's not what the price guide says . . ."

The magazines and books are guides only, not promises that everyone will charge that price. Remember, the prices listed are what dealers want you to *pay*. If you want to *sell* a listed item, a dealer may want to pay you only half of "book." After all, the dealer will want to sell it to someone else at the listed price—and make a little money for his trouble.

Listen and learn. Dealers and collectors will reveal wrong turns they've made. Remember, no matter what stock car racing memorabilia costs, questions are always free.

ONE CAR'S PAIN CAN BE A COLLECTOR'S GAIN. HERE'S PROOF OF SOME PAINT SWAPPIN' BY DRIVER JEREMY MAYFIELD.
(IMAGE COURTESY OF DAVE PHILLIPS)

6

COLLECTIBLES... HERE?

So a trip to the Daytona 500 might be as possible for you as a vacation at the White House?

Collectors just getting started with stock car racing memorabilia sometimes worry about living too far from the tracks. But if you think you have to go to the races for collectibles, think again. Chances are, the collectibles are trying to come to you.

Sure, collectors who live in North Carolina—the state filled with tracks and team shops—are going to see the most choices in racing collectibles. Likewise, anyone from a city with a track or speedway will get more exposure to motorsports memorabilia. But you don't have to be a "Did Not Finish" in the race for collectibles, no matter where you live. Just remember, you may not find something unless you're looking for it.

Be prepared. Make a list of the primary and secondary sponsors of your favorite drivers. Watch or read about current races, because companies enter and leave NASCAR sponsorship throughout the season. The names change.

DRIVER ERNIE IRVAN RETIRED FOLLOWING THE 1999 SEASON, ENDING A 12-YEAR CAREER. ACTION HONORED IRVAN WITH A SPECIALLY-DESIGNED M&M'S MILLENNIUM PAINT SCHEME, FEATURED ON THIS 1:25-SCALE DIE-CAST CREW CAB, TRAILER, AND RACE CAR.
(IMAGE COURTESY OF ACTION PERFORMANCE COMPANIES, INC. USED WITH PERMISSION.)

And the names are many. Even though Dupont has held naming rights for Jeff Gordon's car and team, the sides and back of the car have carried additional sponsor names, such as Pedigree Dog Food or Kellogg's cereal. These names can be clues to collectibles.

Food for Thought

For example, when you notice the Kellogg's logo in a race, head to the cereal aisle of your grocery store. Kellogg's put its Corn Flakes team car on a box of the product in 1991. Surviving specimens (without the cereal) bring fifty dollars and up. The promotion's popularity helped assure Kellogg's continued sponsorship.

After the Corn Flakes brand issued more than fifty different racing box fronts, General Mills cereals answered by picturing Johnny Benson on Cheerios boxes in 1998. Richard Petty and Dale Earnhardt, who had first appeared on Kellogg's boxes, later graced Wheaties fronts. The racing battle between the two cereal giants was in high gear by the 2000 season.

When you read in a hobby magazine or see on a Web site that a new commemorative cereal box will be issued, copy that information down. If you can't find it at the grocery store, ask to see a store manager. (Clerks or shelf stockers may not know

ROBERT YATES RACING TEAM DRIVERS DALE JARRETT AND RICKY RUDD PARTNERED WITH ACTION PERFORMANCE AND THE UNITED STATES ARMED FORCES TO COMMEMORATE THE FIRST MEMORIAL DAY CELEBRATION OF THE 21ST CENTURY WITH "A TRIBUTE TO FREEDOM IN THE MILLENNIUM." THEY WERE TWO OF FIVE DRIVERS FROM NASCAR'S WINSTON CUP SERIES WHO DROVE SPECIALLY DESIGNED MILITARY-THEMED PAINT SCHEMES IN THE MAY 28 RACE AT CHARLOTTE.
(IMAGE COURTESY OF ACTION PERFORMANCE COMPANIES, INC. USED WITH PERMISSION.)

about future orders.) Sometimes, you may need an adult to help get your question asked, because store employees can get quite busy.

Don't forget, the grocery store wants to make money—your money. If store managers know that race fans would buy a product because of a special package front, they try hard to stock the product. A good store employee will say, "I'll check with that company's representative. Watch the shelf. I should know in a week."

Of course, some companies are slow to realize that collecting consumers live everywhere. There are still corporate executives who believe that race fans live only in the southeastern United States. These companies issue promotions regionally—that is, to certain states or cities where tracks are located. General Mills used to be guilty of such ideas with its Wheaties sports boxes. However, boxes sometimes can be ordered online now from Big G, even if the company isn't offering the commemorative cereal to stores in your area.

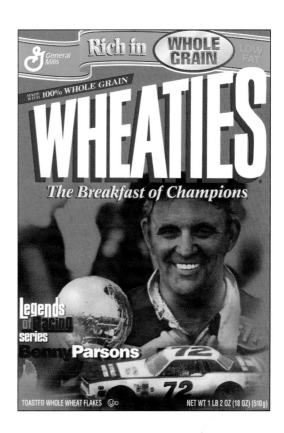

In 2000, Wheaties issued four "Legends of Racing" boxes, picturing Benny Parsons, Richard Petty, Ned Jarrett, and Cale Yarborough. General Mills sold the boxes online to collectors in areas where stores didn't carry the special issues. Many collectors stored the boxes empty and flat. (Image courtesy of General Mills)

Mailing for Memorabilia

Whether your driver's sponsor makes cereal, soft drinks, or detergent, always look carefully at product boxes. Mail-in offers abound. Buy two packages of the product, send in each UPC (universal price code—the lined bars that tell computers the price), and get a unique collectible. Cards and die-casts are favorite premiums offered by companies. These items may cost a dollar or more, often to pay for shipping and handling, but dealers are likely to ask even more for the same collectible in the future.

Why? Because it took work to acquire the item. Some fans may not wish to eat, drink, or wash with that much product—or with that particular product. When money alone won't get the collectible, fewer of the items might be seen in public after the mail-in promotion ends.

No offers on product boxes? Keep looking around. Sometimes, free posters appear on an end-aisle display in a supermarket. If the sign reads "Free," then take one. "Free With Purchase" means you have to buy the product of the race-team sponsor. Still, you don't have to mail in and wait eight to twelve weeks for your collectible.

Next, take a close look at that fancy product display. Often, collectors stand and drool over those life-size cardboard standups of drivers. Wouldn't that be a great addition to a collection? But it would be impossible for a regular person to get something like that—wouldn't it?

Maybe. Maybe not. Some companies require that the stores give back the standups after the promotion. Other stores will sell the displays or donate them to charity auctions. But that huge cardboard cutout of Terry Labonte could die in a recycling bin just because no one bothered to find a home for it.

IN JULY 1998, ACTION PERFORMANCE AND JOE GIBBS RACING HELPED PROMOTE THE FILM *SMALL SOLDIERS*. BOBBY LABONTE'S CAR WAS ADORNED WITH A PAINT SCHEME HIGHLIGHTING THE FILM'S LOGO AND CHARACTERS. (IMAGE COURTESY OF ACTION PERFORMANCE COMPANIES, INC. USED WITH PERMISSION.)

Asking Is Free

As soon as the standup appears, ask the store manager about acquiring it. (It wouldn't hurt to bring an adult from your family who is doing the weekly shopping.) Ask if you can have the standup when the sale ends or when the promotion will be changed. Write your name and address down and offer it to the manager. Maybe the manager could tape your name on the back of the cardboard as a "Saved For" note.

Ad It Up

Television can help you in a quest for store advertisements. If current commercials show a driver selling a product, it's likely that a big ad campaign is going on, complete with local tie-ins. If no standups or posters show up around the product in your nearest store, maybe the manager has decided not to use them. Ask about it—but be specific. Give the name of the product and the driver you're looking for. Asking, "Do you have any stuff picturing NASCAR teams that I can have?" may be too vague. Instead try, "Did Kellogg's send any display advertising picturing NASCAR driver Terry Labonte?"

And remember that grocery-store employees aren't the only ones who can help. Watch for other uniforms in the market. Have you ever spotted a delivery driver, such as the Pepsi-Cola person, stocking the shelves with race-friendly products? These store visitors are company workers who help stock their own company's products on shelves in the snack-food aisle and other store sections. Their shirts may even look a little like the fire suits and uniforms worn by the race team their brand sponsors.

They are busy. They have to get to many stores in a day. But practice a fast introduction. "Hi! I am a big fan of Jeff Gordon and the Pepsi team. I collect. Will the driver or car be pictured on any products soon?"

The odds aren't great that the worker will have something to give you on the spot. But sometimes, you might be offered a driver standup or a banner the store doesn't have room to display. Or the delivery worker might have some posters, postcards, or other giveaways.

Beyond the Supermarket

Other businesses in your town have connections to race teams, too. Auto-repair stores sell motor oil. Logically enough, many motor-oil companies sponsor race teams.

Companies making other parts, like car batteries, might be other sponsors.

From TV commercials or the Internet, it's possible to learn about some sponsoring products. When you know what a company sells, you can look it up in the yellow pages in your town and see if there's a local connection. For instance, consider these sponsors of drivers during the 2000 season:

Michael Waltrip—Nations Rent

Joe Nemechek—Oakwood Homes

Brett Bodine—Ralphs Foods

Elliott Sadler—CITGO

Bodine's sponsor is a West Coast supermarket chain with more than 400 stores. Sadler's CITGO is a gas/service station with 15,000 locations across the country. Oakwood Homes, sponsoring Nemechek, sells factory-built, prefabricated homes. And Waltrip was sponsored by a company that rents construction equipment.

All of this information can be uncovered at a public library. Reference departments have books that list corporations with an explanation of their products and services. Best of all, the books often provide addresses and names of company leaders.

Sending to Sponsors

Finding the name of a customer-service director or specific company representative will help your chances of getting a response by mail. If you address your envelope: "Tide Detergent, Cincinnati, Ohio," anyone at the company could open your letter—and it could be someone with little knowledge of the company's NASCAR connections.

Pick one name out and address your letter to that company executive. Your letter might read something like this:

Dear _____,

I am a fan of (driver) and the (team name) team. Thank you for sponsoring this team. I looked up some facts about your company. I didn't know if you had a store where I live in (your town and state).

I have a racing collection. I would like it if you could send me something that shows your car to add to my collection. Thank you.

Sincerely,
(Your Name)

Your letter proves that NASCAR's appeal is far-reaching and that a sponsor can find potential customers across the country. This encouragement to the company may bring you a collectible reward. A photo or poster might be a common reply. But companies could send something more. After all, you would be a free, walking billboard if the company sent you a T-shirt or cap. You would advertise their product wherever you went!

Be prepared for protests from adults concerning certain sponsors. Jimmy Spencer's 2000 Busch team was sponsored by Zippo Lighters. Miller Beer continued to sponsor Rusty Wallace. Dale Earnhardt Jr. was backed by Budweiser. Coors Light was Sterling Marlin's sponsor. Even the major racing divisions, Winston Cup and Busch Grand National, are the respective namesakes of a cigarette company and a brewery.

What Can't Kids Collect?

You may see posters and promotional items simply as racing collectibles. You may focus on the sport or the driver. But some adults worry that you'll want to drink beer or smoke cigarettes because of the drivers and their sponsors. What can you do if parents and other grown-ups believe that store memorabilia are tempting you to do wrong?

Without speaking rudely, have an explanation prepared. Can you convince a store manager that you won't commit crimes, that you don't want the beer, just the poster from the beer sponsor? Are you ready to explain why you love stock car racing?

Consider this conversation:

Store Employee: Hey, kids can't buy cigarettes or drink beer. It's against the law. You shouldn't be looking at that stuff.

Kid Collector: But having a NASCAR collection isn't illegal. I have a collection of cards, die-cast cars, and other memorabilia from all sponsors. I'm glad that companies help pay for racing. But I won't break the law to thank them. I'm a fan of the drivers, not the products.

Being able to explain what racing and racing collectibles means to you is important. Who knows? You might build a "pit crew" of people in your town to help you build a winning collection faster and cheaper than you could by yourself.

SHOW CARS COLLECT MEMORIES

In horse racing, old horses are put out to pasture to slow down or to do other things. In NASCAR, old cars slow down, too—but they still hit the road.

Meet the show cars.

Show cars travel to groceries, malls, and department stores to give fans a chance to see real race cars up close and personal. Inside and out, from the paint schemes to the engines, show cars are the same as the cars that hit the tracks. Some show cars saw active race duty. Other show cars were built to race, but may never have seen action after a displeased driver's trial run. Nearly all show cars come with company representatives who can answer any questions about the car on display.

Show-car representatives are in charge of delivering the vehicle to its appearance location. The car gets to ride in its own trailer, without starting the engine, which keeps it clean for an inside-and-out inspection by fans.

THE PINNACLE "PORTRAITS" SET NOTES THAT MANY DRIVERS HAVE ADDED "TM" TO THEIR NAMES—REGISTERED TRADEMARKS. LIKE ANY COMPANY LEGALLY PROTECTING A FAMOUS BRAND, DRIVERS WANT TO MAKE SURE THAT NO ONE ELSE MAKES A PROUCT— AND MONEY—USING THEIR NAMES. (COURTESY OF PLAYOFF CORPORATION)

Some show-car specialists are former pit-crew members, or have driven transporters or motor homes for drivers or crew chiefs. Sometimes, a retired husband and wife become a show-car team.

Fans often love to have their pictures taken by a *real* race car. Getting on-the-spot answers about racing is fun, too. To top off a visit, show-car helpers often bring free collectibles for everyone.

Door Prizes

In the 1990s, for example, the Tide racer was a common sight at malls and supermarkets. A fan-club application of driver Ricky Rudd was a standard handout to everyone who visited. Hero cards (photos of the driver and car with a biography and some

ACTION PERFORMANCE CREATED A SUPERMAN-THEMED DESIGN FOR JEFF GORDON'S MAY 22, 1999, RACE IN CHARLOTTE, N.C. (IMAGE COURTESY OF ACTION PERFORMANCE COMPANIES, INC. USED WITH PERMISSION.)

statistics on the back), posters, and even die-cast replicas were given away. However, some stores wanted fans to buy the detergent in order to obtain the die-cast. Such features are still part of the show-car experience. Some current show-car presentations provide magnets that combine pictures and schedules of the upcoming NASCAR season as free souvenirs.

Roush Racing fields teams for six different drivers in NASCAR. Ken Koch, show-car manager for Roush Racing, said his company had a total of twenty-five show vehicles. Koch encouraged fans to check team and sponsor Web sites, such as www.roushracing.com, which might list upcoming show-car visits across the country.

"We operate on a 200-day-a-year schedule, which includes time off and travel days," he said. The Roush Web site noted that their show vehicles have made more than 12,000 appearances, from England to Alaska.

Show cars rack up a lot of mileage. For instance, the Band-Aid showcars, each painted just like the one driven by Michael Waltrip in 2000, made 100 appearances at stores where the Band-Aid product was sold.

Fans have started collecting scrap metal and even hoods from their favorite racers. A show car might be an ultimate collectible—although many hobbyists might not have room for such a treasure. The next best thing is to meet a four-wheeled warrior up close and scoop up all the free memorabilia.

8

SIGNS OF THE TIMES

The drivers and team members in NASCAR are famed throughout the sports world. No other sport has such high numbers of happy signers. But when the number of fans wanting autographs is high, too, even the most willing signers find that signing autographs becomes a numbers game.

How many times could you sign your name neatly in one hour? How long would it take you to sign your name a thousand times? And who thinks that only a thousand fans at a race would want Bill Elliott's autograph? Even the fastest driver finds that he is not fast enough to please all the fans waiting for signatures.

That's why drivers often sign on the move, walking from the garage to another area of the track. Kids tease friends about not being able to walk and chew gum at the same time. Drivers have to walk fast and write their names at the same time!

Even an announced, organized autograph session can be a letdown. If a driver has agreed to sit down to sign for an hour, he may be trying to speed through a line of

AUTOGRAPHS GIVE A COLLECTIBLE
A DRIVER'S QUIET APPROVAL.
HERE, NO ONE WOULD DOUBT
THAT THIS QUARTER-PANEL WAS
FROM A MIKE SKINNER CAR. IF IT
WASN'T, WHY WOULD HE SIGN IT?
(IMAGE COURTESY OF DAVE PHILLIPS)

Is this a paint scrape on race-used sheet metal? Not really. driver Tony Stewart autographed the car's remains. (Image courtesy of Dave Phillips)

fans. He may do little more than mumble hellos as he stares down, trying to sign his name quickly. After all, some fans may judge the driver only on the number of fans left waiting in line when he has to leave, not on the five hundred autographs he cranked out.

Mail Call

Mail is the best answer. With a self-addressed, stamped envelope, it's possible to get one or two cards signed by virtually anyone in NASCAR. A short, polite letter is all you need.

And if you don't have any cards, don't worry. Request an autographed photo from a driver's fan club by sending a 9-by-12-inch (23-by-30-cm) self-addressed, stamped envelope. This should have two stamps on it, because envelopes that big cost extra. Mark your SASE: "Photo: Please Do Not Bend," just to be safe.

When collectors write to drivers in care of their team shop, the mail is sometimes forwarded to fan-mail secretaries who help with the reply. That's one thing fan clubs do best. You can think of fan clubs as driver-fan connectors.

In the past, autographed index cards have been popular. They could be framed later, showcased with a photo, program, or other item. But now, drivers fear the inexpensive, innocent item could be a tool of criminals. One simple autograph could make a counterfeit collectible look real.

NASCAR drivers have followed the lead of some stars from other sports in a recent hobby trend. Some sports celebrities now fear their autograph could be easily reproduced and misused if signed on a blank index card. Jimmy Spencer's fan-club assistants were some of the first to send notes back to collectors saying the driver will not autograph blank, white items.

SIX-YEAR-OLD FAN KYLE PHILLIPS GOT A CHANCE TO SEE DRIVER JEREMY MAYFIELD DISPLAYING ONE OF HIS TOP TALENTS—SIGNING AUTOGRAPHS! (IMAGE COURTESY OF DAVE PHILLIPS)

Other drivers shared Spencer's worry. Drivers treat their autographs as registered trademarks, just like the golden arches symbol for McDonald's. In fact, facsimiles of their autographs appear above driver's-side doors. These are as official as a nameplate on the door of the school principal's office.

T-shirt makers who make deals to produce official souvenir driver shirts will ask the driver for an autograph. The autograph goes on a plain white piece of paper, then is reproduced for an authentic copy of the signature on the T-shirt design. Anyone making illegal driver T-shirts without driver, team owner, and sponsor permission (and without sharing profits with them) could figure out how to re-create a driver's autograph on shirts or other unlicensed products.

By Mail to Packs?

Since 1992, racing-card sets have included randomly inserted autographs. Some drivers autographed as few as fifty cards per set. Although collectors enjoy the belief that these autographs are guaranteed authentic, collectors might be shocked at how some companies have obtained the signatures.

Often, the companies pay the drivers for autographs. They send the drivers an agreed-upon number of the cards. Then the driver may include a signed agreement that says, "I guarantee these autographs were signed by me."

In the end, there's little difference between the signed autograph a fan gets back in the mail and the autographs a card company bought. Although the insert card autograph was produced in a limited amount, that doesn't prove that anyone anywhere would have to pay $50 to $100 for Tony Stewart's autograph on any item.

Limited Supply

When 19-year-old driver Adam Petty died in a wreck during a practice lap at a New Hampshire Speedway early in the 2000 season, the message was sent again to autograph collectors. Stock car racing can be a dangerous sport. The participants of NASCAR might not be available to sign autographs forever. While Adam Petty had continued his family tradition of signing generously during his few years as a professional driver, his death reinforced the cold, hard rule of supply and demand to hobbyists. Values for the signatures of Petty, and all deceased drivers, climb quickly. Those same signatures could have come easily for a few minutes of letter writing and a couple of stamps.

Either in person or in the mail, don't limit your autograph seeking to drivers. Team owners like Richard Childress and Jack Roush have given drivers and crew chiefs the chance to win. Crew chiefs are gaining fame as leaders and planners, the same as a coach who shapes and guides a team to a championship. NASCAR history is expanding to include these winners, even if they didn't make their marks behind the wheel. Few collectors think to ask for these autographs. These signatures not only might be easier for hobbyists to acquire, but these autographs may also be the rarest gems in a collection someday.

TEAM SHOPS: HIDEAWAYS OR SHOW HOMES?

Every superhero has a super-hideaway. Batman has the Batcave. Superman has his Fortress of Solitude. For race teams, it's the race shop.

At one time, a "shop" was where a team kept its cars and spare parts. Mechanics worked there. The name means little these days. Many race teams have made their shops into a mission control, a headquarters, and a museum.

Want to see trophies, memorabilia from past seasons, and photos galore? And cars, cars, cars? Try a shop like that of Bill Elliott's team in Statesville, North Carolina. Elliott's museum displays artifacts from his 25-plus years in NASCAR. But very few shops still allow fans to stroll through selected areas, with a chance to talk to the specialists who make and fix race cars. Fans aren't allowed to roam through Elliot's shops, but they do offer viewing windows. Except, of course, for the gift shop, a popular feature of many headquarters such as Elliott's.

Check a motorsports periodical like *Winston Cup Scene* and you're bound to find a classified that sells addresses of NASCAR team shops throughout North Carolina. However, that same information is free in many formats. Try www.raceshops.com first. Web master Jack Cathey publishes an annual book with addresses and directions to shops, along with detailed reviews on which spots provide the best visits and value for fans and collectors. Although he sells the book, Cathey provides sample information for free. Cathey's reviews are fact-filled fun. For instance, he described the new shop of Dale Earnhardt Inc. (DEI), which houses Dale Earnhardt Jr.'s team. Cathey called it the shop "Garage Mahal," comparing it to India's famed palace the Taj Mahal.

The best team shops can please both fans and collectors. "Many times, while you are visiting a shop, you will see a driver," Cathey said. "When they have time, most drivers are glad to pose for a picture and/or autograph something." Cathey stressed that at times drivers *are* too busy to interact with fans. "But many people think they can't ask a driver—and they can."

Even without a driver present, collectors don't have to leave empty-handed. "Many of the shops offer free items, such as the cards that have the driver and car pictured on them," Cathey said. "Also, some of the shops have free items such as [associate] sponsor decals. [Some] of my favorite free/low-cost items are lug nuts. The teams don't typically reuse them, and kids just love to have something from a real race car."

Cathey revealed another free treat for fans. "The other thing people enjoy when they visit shops is watching a pit crew practice. Most teams practice either around lunch or late in the day. Some practice every day; most practice at least two to three times each week. Fans can call ahead, or ask when they get to a shop."

What does the well-traveled Web master consider the best buys from team shops? "Probably the best low-cost and unique stuff is at Richard Petty's Museum," which unfortunately costs to enter, Cathey said. "They usually have a whole table full of stuff like pistons, brake shoes, spark plugs, and other real race-car items for sale. Richard Childress [team owner for Dale Earnhardt] does the same thing, but the parts are often autographed and cost a bit more."

Some North Carolina towns have chambers of commerce or tourism departments that tell the world about their race shops. After all, a fan who comes to town to see a shop might spend money on food and other purchases.

But a few team owners don't want to be tourist attractions for fans. They want to keep their shopwork as secret as possible and just concentrate on turning out winning cars. Petty Enterprises, in Randleman, North Carolina, housed the Kyle Petty and John Andretti teams in 2000. Fans were charged three dollars for admission to the museum. However, the shop was off limits, without a single window for visitors to peek into.

Avid NASCAR collectors find memories and more by visiting team race shops. Cars and engines are made and fixed in these garages. Jack Cathey publishes a travel guide profiling all shops that welcome fans. (Courtesy of Jack Cathey and www.raceshops.com)

Pay, or Stay Away?

Some team owners don't even release their shop addresses in hopes that fan mail will be sent to the fan club instead. A few have justified their secrecy by saying that mail can get greasy and ruined in a car shop.

Whether you want to take your chances writing for an autograph, or whether you go for a tour, remember that drivers don't live at their team shops. Drivers spend time testing new engines and cars at tracks, then make appearances around the country for their sponsors before finally snatching a moment at home with their families. But even when the drivers aren't in the shop, fans can learn about their favorite team from the folks behind the scenes. The appendix on pages 66 and 67 of this book lists all known race shops, along with their drivers.

FANS LOVE THOSE CLUBS

Maybe you read in the paper that a new driver on the local track is from Missouri. "Hey," you think, "my dad's from Missouri." You start noticing this driver's name when you read. You start cheering for him at the track. One night, you notice another fan holding a sign with your driver's name on it. You go over and chat. Someone else joins the conversation. That's how a fan club begins.

But as the number of fans grows, so do club activities. Many of today's fan clubs are clearinghouses for information about the driver. You want a driver's autograph? His fan club is the place to write. Fan club workers—volunteers or paid staff—sort mail. They help drivers keep organized, so items sent for autographing get put back in the right envelopes.

Even race fans who aren't chasing autographs should consider writing to a driver's fan club with a self-addressed, stamped envelope. Stickers, schedules, photos... the fan clubs may give more free goodies to collectors than any other resource.

Fan clubs will send small souvenirs to any fan, not just club members. But for dues-paying members, the treats just get bigger and better.

Newsletters may be circulated once yearly or monthly. These papers offer exclusive photos of the driver and race team. Many newsletters contain columns written by the driver and team members. Best of all, the newsletter will detail collectibles related to that driver and team.

Some fan clubs even commission member-exclusive card sets or die-cast cars. While these collectibles may not be free, they won't be sold to nonmembers.

Dues Depend

The costs of fan-club membership vary wildly depending on how many services and collectibles are provided each year. And the cost doesn't always depend on how famous the driver is. Dues in 2000 for racing legend Richard Petty's Fan Club cost only $10 per person. On the other end of the money meter were fan clubs for Roush drivers Mark Martin or Jeff Burton. They cost $25 annually. Many of the $20-and-up memberships for clubs include a souvenir T-shirt picturing the driver and car.

Luckily, nearly all fan clubs offer big discounts for family memberships. For instance, in the 2000 season the Kenny Wallace Fan Club dues cost $14 for one fan or $16 for the whole family.

Perhaps one of the biggest perks of membership is the in-person contact at fan-club meetings, known as "Meet and Greet" sessions. Not only do fans get to meet *their* driver, but they also meet other fans that share their interest. The personal contact may also allow for picture taking, question-and-answer sessions, and autographs.

Sometimes, fan clubs are operated by professional companies. Notice how fan clubs for the Earnhardts, Dale Jarrett, and Rusty Wallace all seem to be sharing space at the same Arizona location? But just because a large company is in charge of a fan club doesn't mean that club is the best.

Small clubs can mean more personal interaction. Often, a smaller fan club is located in the driver's hometown and operated by friends or family members. Usually, these organizers are unpaid. They work out of devotion to that driver and team.

Wallace and Wallace

The Kenny Wallace Fan Club is family-operated. Kim Wallace, the driver's wife, is a behind-the-scenes star who has spent years keeping Kenny's fans happy. "Kenny's been racing for twelve years. We've had the fan club for ten years," she said. "We have a large following, especially in the Northeast. Other drivers have companies running their fan clubs. But I think we'd lose something. There's a personal touch here." That personal touch remains, even though "We've gone from two hundred members the first year to more than four thousand members now," Wallace said.

A family that buys a membership to Kenny's fan club receives four newsletters a year, an autographed photo, and a membership kit that includes twenty-three to twenty-five pieces, such as earplugs or window clings for cars. "We're always thinking about what would be useful for fans at a race," Wallace said. When the sponsors provide souvenirs like extra team jackets, Mrs. Wallace ensures that contests make the bonuses available to members. She oversees other surprises, too. For instance, Kenny calls one fan club member per month to say "Happy Birthday."

"I'm a mom of three," said Kim Wallace. "I put that same [kind of] heart and soul in this fan club. We have a picture board here called 'The Kenny Wallace Fan Club Family.' We show members and their collections," Wallace said. "Fans send pictures of how they painted strollers, lawn mowers—you name it—all to match the paint scheme on Kenny's car. I have what I'd call my own little museum. I've kept all the creations fans have sent."

Wallace helps fans share with each other. "We have an office with pictures [from Kenny's career] on the walls. Fan-club members can come in and sit and talk," she said. "I've saved everything: his helmets, his uniforms, his shoes. They can see it all."

Clubs Checklist Collectibles

Likewise, members help the Wallace family keep track of all the new collectibles depicting Kenny. "It's impossible for us to know [all the memorabilia Kenny's pictured on]. Drivers have marketing assistants who'll see that the driver is pictured properly and that the sponsor logos are correct," Kim Wallace said. "[But] sometimes at an autograph signing session, I'll sit behind him and he'll see a new card. He may say to me, 'Look at this!' It's a card we've never seen before. I may have only one-tenth of the collectibles on him."

One of the best collectibles that fans can own is the memory of a face-to-face meeting with their hero. Kim Wallace knows that. She expected 900 to 1,000 fans to show up at the next meeting. "At fan club meetings, Kenny's there. Two hours, five hours—he never complains," she said.

Does it work? "We receive letters from fans who attend his personal appearances. They'll write, 'He answered my question. He looked up and greeted me. He made me feel like I was the only one there,'" she said. "At a two-hour session, Kenny can do about 570 autographs. He could do more if he just scribbled his name or didn't visit with everyone. But he has a very legible autograph. It may look like lots of loops, but you can see each of the letters."

Like a talented crew chief, Kim Wallace works with her husband to please the floods of autograph seekers. "We receive ten-thousand pieces of mail per month. We'll set all letters aside for Kenny to read. Members get their autograph requests answered first. We put in fan-club applications when Kenny signs for nonmembers," she said.

Sorting the Signing

"By computer, the fan-club director tracks the address of whoever requested the autograph. After the first request, we'll send a nice letter back that explains Kenny's limited time. We send their items back unsigned. The letter explains that they received autographs back once, and that he can sign regularly only for members," she said.

Kenny devotes one day a month solely to the fan club and its members. With a schedule of thirty-two races and sixty personal appearances for his sponsors, he's busy throughout the year. (The Kenny Wallace Fan Club and other club addresses are provided in the Appendix of this book.)

COLLECTING FOR A CAUSE

Stock car racing collectibles can make hobbyists into heroes. In Marshalltown, Iowa, the Woodbury Elementary School highlights each school year with its "Stay On the Right Track" program. Learning about racing is a fun way to learn math, social studies, and other subjects.

Each school year at Woodbury ends with a school assembly and special guests. Drivers from the local dirt track come in uniform, with their cars to display and their autographs to share. Their "right track" messages include staying in school and avoiding drugs.

When fourth-grade teacher Bart Mason (who admits he's an "odds and ends" collector) came up with the idea, he asked Woodbury teaching staff member Kim Ladehoff and her race-fan husband, Mike, to help. The threesome began contacting NASCAR teams and sponsors for donations.

Woodbury isn't a school with a lot of money. The original hope was to get souvenir T-shirts for all the students. But then, one-of-a-kind donations started coming

An autographed, race-used helmet by Kyle Petty shows that the radio and microphone used to communicate with the pit crew is still attached. Note how sponsors even consider a driver's head to be potential advertising space.
(Image courtesy of Dave Phillips)

in, such as a piece of sheet metal from one of Jeff Gordon's wrecks. "We [realized] that if we sold the memorabilia, it could benefit all students, not just one," Mason said.

That's how the annual Woodbury charity auction was born. Mason said that for the 2000 event, the Woodbury team sent out between 600 and 700 letters asking NASCAR teams and sponsors for donations. "We received between 100 and 150 responses," he continued. Combined with local support and sponsors, the auction offered 400 collectibles for sale. Money raised would go toward playground improvements and buying sports equipment.

Nevertheless, finding teams to donate is like a race, Mason said. "Some drivers, like Jeff Gordon, choose to support specific charities, like leukemia research. Some teams will only donate to charities in their own state," he said.

Hobbyists Helping Hobbyists

Some collectors and dealers made their own donations to Woodbury Elementary. "We get outdated memorabilia donated sometimes," Mason said. "Some people don't want die-cast or collectibles showing drivers with old sponsors."

The most popular item at the 2000 auction was a cap that had been autographed by three generations of racing Pettys. The autograph of Adam Petty, along with father Kyle and grandfather Richard, turned the item into a $230 seller. Sadly, Adam had died in a May racetrack practice just before the auction, making his autograph a sought-after collectible.

The third annual event attracted 85 bidders, some traveling to central Iowa from surrounding states. "Near the end, you could find bargains," Mason said. A 1:24 scale die-cast of Dale Earnhardt Jr.'s AC Delco car brought $25, while price guides listed the same car near $100. But bidders had already exhausted their budgets. With fewer able to compete for the final items, the remaining choice collectibles went cheap.

Several NASCAR stars, as big as life, made appearances. Sort of. Numerous stores and sponsors donated life-size cardboard standups. A Coca-Cola display showing Dale Earnhardt topped out at $50. Most standees sold in the $20 to $30 range.

At the end of the evening, more than $5,000 had been raised to help a school and its students. Thanks to the power of stock car racing memorabilia, the winner's circle kept growing in Marshalltown, Iowa.

UNCOMMON USES FOR COMMONS

Sometimes, saving every racing card you've ever gotten seems like a great idea. Thinking about all of those cards going up in value is fun. But the hope that all your cards will make you rich someday is a huge expectation. The fact is, many of the cards you acquire in packs will be commons, forever seen as low-value, unwanted cards by everyone except set collectors.

The cards are called commons because they're everywhere. They're common. They ooze out from under your bed and make your bedroom shelves sag from strain. Maybe they show cars without identifying the driver. Maybe they show Jack the jackman or some other pit-crew member from the 1990s that nobody remembers.

That's not to say you can't find great uses for commons. For instance, use your commons for . . .

Halloween: Yes, most kids like getting candy for trick-or-treats. However, there's no reason you can't provide a few motorsports cards gathered in plastic wrap for each October visitor.

Crafts: Who wouldn't laugh to see their school picture portrait pasted on the body of a Rainbow Warrior team member? Get out your commons and try using them to decorate posters, homemade birthday cards, homework assignments, and more.

Garage Sales: Setting up a table at a rummage or tag sale won't bring in lots of collectors willing to pay price-guide rates for rookie cards or inserts. Garage-sale shoppers most often hunt for quantity, not quality. Offer them bundles of commons displayed in sandwich bags. Put a driver's card from a popular team on top of the pile to shine through the wrapping. Try different sizes of commons bags to sell—ten cards

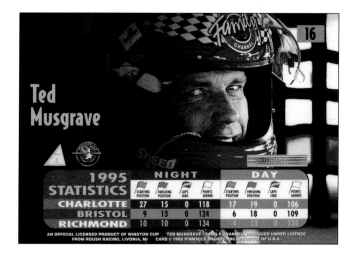

for a quarter or fifty cards for a dollar. Experiment with low prices, and you may be selling cards by the pound soon. Some sale visitors might even ask if you would like to buy their motorsports cards—that could be a deal for you!

Your Family: Do you have a little brother or sister who always wants to mess with your collection? Instead of screaming for help to keep your star cards from being crushed, use your commons to protect your hobby. Offer a pile of them to your younger siblings as a present. Explain that they have their own collections now. Tell them you might trade them other cards if they take care of the first ones they've been given. Spend the money to get them a cardboard storage box so the cards can be kept safe. You can teach a younger family member about the right ways to collect, while keeping your cards at a safer distance.

Your Town: Ask teachers at your school if there are any ways that your extra cards could be used in their classrooms. Cards teach geography (where the teams and drivers are from or where races are held), mathematics (speed, an engine's horsepower, gas mileage, following the contenders for the points championship), and writing (some cards seem to tell a driver's whole life in fifty words or less). Your teachers know how popular motorsports cards are. Any time teachers can use a current, popular item to help teach, it makes their job easier.

Donations: Find out if the nearest hospital would welcome your cards. Maybe a teacher, an adult from your church, or an older family member can call for information on how to donate cards for sick kids. Ask your friends if they would add to the donation. Maybe a group of collector/customers could ask the nearest hobby shop to match their gift, providing twice as many cards for kids who need cheering up.

No matter what you decide to do with your extra cards, remember that financial value is only one benefit your hobby can bring. Sharing your interest with others brings the best, longest-lasting value of all.

A MOTORSPORTS HOBBY MAKEOVER

Too much! Too fast! Just like drivers, stock car racing collectors may spin out at any time, overwhelmed by too many hobby choices.

Can you make changes if your money starts to disappear, or if you're getting bored with one type of collectible? Until crew chiefs start working for collectors to develop winning strategies, here are suggestions that could help any level of motorsports collector.

Redefine Your Collection

Suppose you're a racing-card collector. Does that mean you can only collect piles of cardboard rectangles? Think of all the sidelines you can find to help showcase the set you're collecting.

Most important is the wrapper or package the cards come in. How many collectors saved wrappers from the first Maxx set in 1988? Cards, no problem. The wrapper? Hard to find. And if it's hard to find, it's fun to look for—and it can even be valuable.

Another reason wrappers are rare is that companies sometimes want wrappers returned. Companies still have mail-in offers that promise special card sets or other collectibles as long as wrappers are mailed in as proof of your product purchase. Collectors who go to the trouble of answering mail-in offers are getting true collectibles. In future years, those wrapper redemption prizes may be more valuable than any of the cards found in the packs—or the wrappers they came in!

Next, check at card shops for what isn't there. Is the dealer throwing out empty boxes that housed racing packs? Did the dealer get posters or shelf displays from a company to advertise its set? Are those display items being used? What will happen when the dealer is done with them? Ask about items you are interested in adding to your own collection. Anything made by the manufacturer of the cards you're collecting should be considered for your collection, especially if the price is right. And free is a very good price!

Don't Laugh at Kid Stuff

Have you asked a police officer if he or she has any cards? Some law-enforcement agencies print "safety" sets of drivers. Card backs feature ideas about how to stay safe and smart, warning against drugs, gangs, and other dangers.

Safety sets are usually available only to kids. The tables were turned in 2000 when the California Highway Patrol offered a safety set for fans over age twenty-one. Racing cards were given to any licensed driver who signed up to be a designated driver, someone who agrees to avoid drinking alcohol so that he or she can drive safely for fans who need a ride.

Cards have been made by other groups to get kids to read more, to study more subjects, and to attend church. Religious groups sometimes print cards with inspirational messages about a driver's faith. Try talking to your teachers, librarians, or youth-group leaders. They might know groups that are making such cards.

In all of these cases, the cards are designed with kids in mind. But even if you don't keep the cards in your own collection, they'll still make great trading material. Adults are often too shy to ask for the cards, or they fail to get them from other adults. Most often, adults can only dream of being given cards free of charge! Sometimes, it's good to be young.

Matter by Mail

Write to companies who are sponsoring teams. If you see in *Beckett Racing* that stores in Florida and Alabama offered a certain collectible, write on! Try the Internet or find a librarian who can get you a reference book listing company addresses. Find the headquarters of the company (*not* the race team) that is sponsoring any regional set. Write your letter something like this:

Dear (fill in company sponsor name),
I am a (number)-year-old fan of the (driver and car number). I was happy to learn your company has sponsored a (die-cast, card set, or other memorabilia).

I'm sorry that none of your businesses are close to where I live. I have no way to be part of your promotion. Is there any way I can obtain one of these great items for my personal collection? Thank you.

Sincerely,
(your name)

This tactic worked in the early 1990s when Corn Flakes put Richard Petty on his first box front. Fans wrote the company in protest when boxes were issued only in a few states. All letters were answered with instructions to send two box tops and fifty cents to a special address. As a result, letter-writing hobbyists got an unassembled box (without cereal), suitable for framing! But because the address wasn't recorded in the hobby media, many collectors missed out on the deal.

Maybe McDonald's is sponsoring a motorsports promotion, but the McDonald's in your town isn't participating. Be creative. See if you can talk to the manager of your local franchise. Explain that you are a regular customer, and you would like help getting the collectible. If you've seen magazine pictures of the card, bring a photocopy of the picture. Maybe that manager is friends with the manager of a store in the area giving the items away.

If not, try sending a cash register slip or product wrapper to the headquarters when you write for more information. You should offer proof that you support that business. Most of all, describe your shopping and eating habits. Does your whole family like the burgers or groceries that the collectible-offering sponsor sells? Add one sentence telling how old you are and how many members of your family use the company's products. Companies know that kids will keep eating the foods and products they choose now for years to come. Even if you aren't a big spender now, companies hope you'll buy their brands in the future. Maybe sending you some free cards will help you make up your mind, no matter where you live.

Love All Leagues

Indy cars. Formula One. Funny car dragsters. Sprint cars. You've always liked NASCAR better. So why should you consider collecting some cards and die-casts from these other leagues? Because one league often leads to another.

Jeff Gordon started as a sprint-car driver. And the sprint-car track in Knoxville, Iowa (site of the yearly National Championships) usually hosts a NASCAR star once a

UNOPENED PACKS ARE COLLECTIBLE. DEALERS KNOW THAT COLLECTORS MAY LIKE THE POSSIBILITY OF FINDING AN AUTOGRAPHED CARD, NO MATTER HOW TOUGH THE ODDS ARE.
(COURTESY OF UPPER DECK COMPANY, LLC)

year for a pre-race autograph session. NASCAR itself even has the Craftsman Truck series. Drivers like Ron Hornaday and Kevin Horvick, rookie stars in the Busch series during the 2000 season, used trucks as a testing ground for their skills.

In 2000, Amoco gas stations offered a choice of two die-casts, just ninety-nine cents with an 8-gallon (30-liter) purchase. Fans could choose either a sprint car or Dave Blaney's Winston Cup car. Many fans may have chosen only one car, or may have stashed away duplicates of the Winston Cup car. But remember: It's possible those drivers from other ranks could join the Winston circuit someday. Collectors can create *complete career* collections. And suppose you miss getting the premium you want. If the price is right, get the unwanted premium to use as trading material.

There are many ways to win a race. Crew chiefs help race teams change when needed, trying new ways to keep up with the pack. No matter what your age or income is, there are ways to keep a winning collection. Don't be afraid to test-drive a new game plan.

AFTER DALE EARNHARDT DIED IN A LAST-LAP CRASH AT THE DAYTONA 500 IN 2001, HOBBYISTS WATCHED THE LAWS OF SUPPLY AND DEMAND RUN WILD.

BEFORE THE RACE WAS OVER THAT SUNDAY IN FEBRUARY, THE INTERNET AUCTION WEB SITE EBAY LISTED FEWER THAN 3,000 EARNHARDT ITEMS FOR SALE. BY WEDNESDAY, THE DAY OF EARNHARDT'S FUNERAL, THE NUMBER HAD SKYROCKETED TO MORE THAN 90,000 ITEMS. AND EMOTIONAL FANS WANTING CARDS AND MEMORABILIA STARTED BUYING AT ANYWHERE FROM FIVE TO TWENTY TIMES THE PREVIOUSLY ESTIMATED VALUES.

THE ONLINE AUCTION ALLOWED VIEWERS TO COMPARE AN ITEM'S PERCEIVED VALUE BEFORE AND AFTER THE ACCIDENT. A 1994 CREASED EARNHARDT POSTCARD, AUTOGRAPHED, WAS POSTED BEFORE THE FATAL WRECK WITH A MINIMUM BID OF $9.99. AFTER THE DRIVER'S DEATH, BIDDERS PROPELLED THE PRICE UP PAST $175!

BECAUSE OF EARNHARDT'S SUPERSTARDOM IN NASCAR'S HOBBY WORLD, FAR MORE ITEMS TO CHOOSE FROM EXISTED FEATURING THE LATE DRIVER. BUT WHILE A DEAD DRIVER COULD NO LONGER SIGN AUTOGRAPHS, SOME HOBBYISTS WONDERED ABOUT THE ULTIMATE VALUE OF EARNHARDT'S SIGNATURES. EARNHARDT HAD BEEN A NASCAR MAINSTAY FOR MORE THAN TWENTY YEARS, SIGNING REGULARLY FOR FANS. ADAM PETTY, THE NINETEEN-YEAR-OLD DRIVER KILLED LESS THAN A YEAR EARLIER, HAD DECADES LESS TIME TO SIGN. THE SUPPLY OF PETTY SIGNATURES WOULD BE THOUSANDS LESS THAN THOSE OF "THE MAN IN BLACK."

Fan Club Addresses

You can write for current membership costs, as well as services and souvenirs, to:

BLAISE ALEXANDER
36 Teakwood Dr.
Tiffin, OH 44883

GLENN ALLEN
P.O. Box 2247
Cornelius, NC 28031

BOBBY ALLISON
6616 Walmsley Blvd.
Richmond, VA 23224

JOHN ANDRETTI
P.O. Box 2104
Davidson, NC 28036

RON BARFIELD
P.O. Box 1508
Dawsonville, GA 30534

JOHNNY BENSON
3102 Bird St. NE
Grand Rapids, MI 49505

JOE BESSEY
2004 Renaissance Blvd.
King of Prussia, PA
19406

RICK BICKLE
7365 Elwood Dr.
Charlotte, NC 28227

DAVE BLANEY
P.O. Box 470142
Tulsa, OK 74147

BRETT BODINE
304 Performance Rd.
Mooresville, NC 28115

GEOFFREY BODINE
P.O. Box 1790
Monroe, NC 28111

TODD BODINE
P.O. Box 2427
Cornelius, NC 28031

JEFF BURTON
Roush Sports Group
235-10 Rolling Hills Rd.
Mooresville, NC 28117

WARD BURTON
3475 Myer Lee Dr.
Winston-Salem, NC 27101

RICK CARELLI
2009 Market St.
Denver, CO 80205

RODNEY COMBS
2601 Forsythe Lane
Concord, NC 28025

STACY COMPTON
P.O. Box 637
Hart, VA 24563

DERRIKE COPE
P.O. Box 12306
Spring, TX 77391

RICKY CRAVEN
P.O. Box 472
Concord, NC 28026

MIKE DILLON
P.O. Box 30414
Winston-Salem, NC 27130

DALE EARNHARDT
4707 E. Baseline Rd.
Phoenix, AZ 85040

DALE EARNHARDT JR.
4707 E. Baseline Rd.
Phoenix, AZ 85040

BILL ELLIOTT
P.O. Box 248
Dawsonville, GA 30534

TIM FEDEWA
P.O. Box 3427
Mooresville, NC 28117

JEFF FULLER
P.O. Box 3336
Mooresville, NC 28117

JEFF GORDON
P.O. Box 515
Williams, AZ 86046

DAVID GREEN
P.O. Box 4821
Archdale, NC 27263

JEFF GREEN
P.O. Box 268
Cornelius, NC 28031

MARK GREEN
P.O. Box 5735
Concord, NC 28207

STEVE GRISSOM
P.O. Box 989
Statesville, NC 28687

BOBBY HILLIN
110 Knob Hill Rd.
Mooresville, NC 28115

RON HORNADAY
P.O. Box 870,
Kannapolis, NC 28082

JIMMY HORTON
P.O. Box 4425
Bethlehem, PA 18018

TOMMY HOUSTON
P.O. Box 5250
Conover, NC 28613

ERNIE IRVAN
703 Performance Rd.
Mooresville, NC 28115

DALE JARRETT
4707 E. Baseline Rd.
Phoenix, AZ 85040

BUCKSHOT JONES
P.O. Box 1612
Duluth, GA 30136

JASON KELLER
P.O. Box 14748
Greensville, SC 29610

MATT KENSETH
10 Water St.
Cambridge, WI 53523

TAMMY JO KIRK
743 Peek Rd.
Dalton, GA 30721

BOBBY LABONTE
4707 E. Baseline Rd.
Phoenix, AZ 85040

TERRY LABONTE
P.O. Box 843
Trinity, N.C. 27370

RANDY LAJOIE
P.O. Box 3478
Westport, CT 06880

KEVIN LEPAGE
159 Bevan Dr.
Mooresville, NC 28115

CHAD LITTLE
P.O. Box 562323
Charlotte, NC 28256

CURTIS MARKHAM
433 Bostwick Lane
Gaithersburg, MD 20878

STERLING MARLIN
1116 W. 7th St., Suite 62
Columbia, TN 38401

MARK MARTIN
Roush Sports Group
235-10 Rolling Hills Rd.
Mooresville, NC 28117

RICK MAST
Route 6, Box 224-A
Lexington, VA 24450

JEREMY MAYFIELD
P.O. Box 2365
Cornelius, NC 28031

TED MUSGRAVE
P.O. Box 1089
Liberty, NC 27298

JERRY NADEAU
P.O. Box 1358
Harrisburg, NC 28075

JOE NEMECHEK
P.O. Box 1131
Mooresville, NC 28115

STEVE PARK
P.O. Box 172
E. Northport, NY 11731

KYLE PETTY
135 Longfield Dr.
Mooresville, NC 28115

RICHARD PETTY
1028 E. 22nd St.
Kannapolis, NC 28083

ROBERT PRESSLEY
P.O. Box 1055
Newport News, VA
23601

RICKY RUDD
P.O. Box 4060
Mooresville, NC 28117

ELLIOTT SADLER
P.O. Box 32
Emporia, VA 23847

HERMIE SADLER
P.O. Box 871
Emporia, VA 28847

ANDY SANTERRE
P.O. Box 994
Harrisburg, NC 28075

JAY SAUTER
P.O. Box 278
516-D River Highway
Mooresville, NC 28115

ELTON SAWYER and
PATTY MOISE
P.O. Box 77919
Greensboro, NC 27417

KEN SCHRADER
P.O. Box 1227
Kannapolis, NC 28082

DENNIS SETZER
P.O. Box 214897
Auburn Hills, MI 48326

MORGAN SHEPERD
P.O. Box 1456
Stow, OH 44224

MIKE SKINNER
Team Lowe's Fan Club
P.O. Box 1111
North Wilkesboro, NC
28656

LAKE SPEED
P.O. Box 499
Danville, WV 25053

JIMMY SPENCER
P.O. Box 1626
Mooresville, NC 28115

JACK SPRAGUE
280 Highway 29 South
Suite 120, Box 173
Concord, NC 28027

BILLY STANDRIDGE
1521 Sulphur Springs Rd.
Shelby, NC 28152

TIM STEELE
1143 24th Ave.
Marne, MI 49435-9716

MIKE STEFANIK
200 Myrtle St., 7th Flr.
New Britain, CT 06053

TONY STEWART
5777 W. 74th St.
Indianapolis, IN 46278

RANDY TOLSMA
610 Performance Rd.
Mooresville, NC 28115

DICK TRICKLE
5415 Vesuvius-Furnace Rd.
Iron Station, NC 28080

BILL VENTURINI
7621 Texas Trail
Boca Raton, FL 33487

KENNY WALLACE
P.O. Box 3050
Concord, NC 28025

MIKE WALLACE
224 Rolling Hills Rd.
Suite 9-A
Mooresville, NC 28115

RUSTY WALLACE
4707 E. Baseline Rd.
Phoenix, AZ 85040

DARRELL WALTRIP
P.O. Box 381
Harrisburg, NC 28075

MICHAEL WALTRIP
P.O. Box 339
Sherills Ford, NC 28673

Race Shops

Below is a list of known race shops, along with their drivers in parentheses:

A. J. Foyt Racing
128 Commercial Dr.
Mooresville, NC 28115
(Ron Hornaday)

Andy Petree Motorsports
P.O. Box 325
908 Upward Rd.
East Flat Rock, NC 28726
(Bobby Hamilton/Joe Nemechek)

Bessey Motorsports
11881 Vance Davis Drive
Charlotte, NC 28269

Bill Davis Racing
301 Old Thomasville Rd.
High Point, NC 27260
(Dave Blaney/Ward Burton)

Brett Bodine Racing
304 Performance Rd.
Mooresville, NC 28115
(Brett Bodine)

Dale Earnhardt, Inc.
1675 Coddle Creek Highway
Mooresville, NC 28115
(Steve Park/Dale Earnhardt Jr./
Michael Waltrip)

Donlavey Racing
5011 Old Midlothian Pike
Richmond, VA 23224
(Hut Stricklin)

Eel River Racing
208 Rolling Hills Rd.
Mooresville, NC 28115
(Kenny Wallace)

Evernham Motorsports
7100 Weddington Rd.
Harrisburg, NC 28075
(Bill Elliott/Casey Atwood)

Fenley/Moore Motorsports
400 N. Fairview Ave.
P.O. Box 2916
Spartanburg, SC 29303

Galaxy Motorsports
217 Rolling Hills Rd.
Mooresville, NC 28117
(Wally Dallenbach)

Ganassi Racing
114 Meadow Hill Circle
Mooresville, NC 28115
(Sterling Marlin)

Haas/Carter Motorsports
2670 Peachtree Rd.
Statesville, NC 28625
(Todd Bodine/Jimmy Spencer)

Hendrick Motorsports
4433 Papa Joe Hendrick Blvd.
P.O. Box 9
Harrisburg, NC 28075
(Jeff Gordon/Jerry Nadeau/
  Terry Labonte/Jimmie Johnson)

Joe Gibbs Racing
13415 Reese Blvd. West
Huntersville, NC 28078
(Tony Stewart / Bobby Labonte)

Joyner-Kersee Racing
633 McWay Drive
High Point, NC 27264

Larry Hedrick Motorsports
2541 Victory Lane
Statesville, NC 28677

LJ Racing
129 Bevan Dr.
Mooresville, NC 28115

MacPherson Motorsports
4200 Stough Rd.
Concord, NC 28027

Marcis Auto Racing
P.O. Box 645
Skyland, NC 28776
(Dave Marcis)

MB2 Motorsports
185 McKenzie Rd.
Mooresville, NC 28115
(Ken Schrader)

MB2 Motorsports
6780 Hudspeth Rd.
P.O. Box 910
Harrisburg, NC 28075
(Johnny Benson)

Melling Racing Enterprises
4366 Triple Crown Dr.
Concord, NC 28075
(Stacey Compton)

Midwest Transit Racing
4909 Stough Rd.
Concord, NC 28027
(Ricky Craven)

Morgan/McClure Motorsports
26502 Newbanks Rd.
Abingdon, VA 24211
(Robby Gordon)

Penske Racing South
136 Knob Hill Rd.
Mooresville, NC 28117
(Rusty Wallace/Ryan Newman)

Penske-Kranefuss Racing
163 Rolling Hills Rd.
Mooresville, NC 28117
(Jeremy Mayfield)

Petty Enterprises
311 Branson Mill Rd.
Randleman, NC 27317
(Kyle Petty/John Andretti/
Buckshot Jones)

PPI Motorsports
3051 First Ave. Court SE
Hickory, NC 28602
(Scott Pruett/Andy Houston)

Quest Motor Racing
103 Center Lane
Huntersville, NC 28078
(Derrike Cope)

Richard Childress Racing
P.O. Box 1189
236 Industrial Dr.
Welcome, NC 27374
(Mike Skinner/Kevin Harrick)

Robert Yates Racing
292 Rolling Hills Rd.
Mooresville, NC 28117
(Rickey Rudd/Dale Jarrett)

Robert Yates Racing
P.O. Box 3185
292 Rolling Hills Rd.
Mooresville, NC 28117
(Ricky Rudd)

Roush Racing
122 Knob Hill Rd.
Mooresville, NC 28115
(Mark Martin / Jeff Burton/
Matt Kenseth, Kurt Busch)

Roush Racing
7050 Aviation Blvd.
Concord, NC 28027
(Chad Little/Matt Kenseth/
Kevin Lepage)

Standridge Racing
1521 Sulphur Springs Rd.
Shelby, NC 28152
(Billy Standridge)

Ultra Motorsports
222 Raceway Dr.
Mooresville, NC 28115

Wood Brothers Racing
21 Performance Dr.
Stuart, VA 24171
(Elliott Sadler)

FOR MORE INFORMATION

Magazines

Beckett Racing and Motorsports Marketplace, 15850 Dallas Parkway, Dallas, TX 75248

This monthly magazine, launched in 1994, is from the company that created the idea of sports-card price guides. This is definitely the pole-sitter of hobby publications.

Racing Collector's Price Guide, 5620 Concord Parkways South, Suite 202, Harrisburg, NC 28075

How could this monthly magazine compete with a powerhouse like *Beckett Racing*? *RCPG* passes the favored magazine on the price-guide lap. And *RCPG* came first, in 1991. It offers an exhaustive list of collectibles every month. While *Beckett* often sticks to cards and die-casts, *RCPG* includes cereal boxes, soft drink cans and bottles, plastic model kits, and track programs. If you have an unusual racing item in need of a value, try here first.

Die Cast Digest, P.O. Box 12510, Knoxville, TN 37912-0510

Another monthly, this magazine delivers more die-cast insight than any other. One page details all the variations in packaging and production of the Racing Champions cars. Price guides are the most detailed, noting production numbers when possible, and how the value has changed from the previous month. And *DCD* will not price new items until the second month they are available, so they can thoroughly study pricing trends before making a value judgment.

Winston Cup Weekly, 120 West Moorehead Street, Suite 320, Charlotte, NC 28202

The majority of *WCW* isn't geared for collectors. Mostly, the weekly newspaper is a mammoth recap of top NASCAR news and statistics. However, changes among team sponsors or licensing deals (when NASCAR gives permission for collectibles makers to create new items) gets reported at record speeds. And the classifieds are unmatched in the motorsports hobby media. Fire suits, sheet metal from wrecked cars, helmets—artifacts that won't show up anywhere else—will be offered here.

Paper Racer, http://www.paperracer.com

Editor-publisher Kenny Brackett is a wealth of information on postcards. He publishes a newsletter and an annual price guide. Write for price details.

Books

Fifty Years of Stock Car Racing: A History of Collectibles and Memorabilia, by Ken Breslauer, foreword by Richard Petty. $24.95 (David Bull Publishing, 1998)

This 144-page softcover may never be found in decent condition. Collectors of all ages and levels are likely to love their copies of this pictorial history to death. Breslauer's book offers more than 200 photos of memorabilia that date back to NASCAR's beginnings in 1947. While not offering a price guide, the book provides explanations of collectibles categories.

Petty's comments are worth a peek, too. A 1964 T-shirt picturing Petty's car and his name was the first souvenir clothing sold to fans. Caps followed. What company made it? No one — the Petty family created their own souvenirs because the limited popularity of NASCAR made attracting outside companies difficult. How times have changed! Always the promoter, racing legend Petty's autographs were found on $59.95 hardcovers of Breslauer's book.

Racing Collectibles and Die-Cast Price Guide #5, $14.95 (Beckett Publications, 2000)

The best part of the 496-page softcover is an alphabetical checklist at no extra cost. When did "Little E" make his motorsports card debut? Dale Earnhardt Jr. first made appearances in card sets in 1994, appearing in the High Gear and Optima XL sets. The latter set, made by Press Pass, included cards of racing siblings, brother Kerry and sister Teresa.

It's all in the Beckett annual, complete with extended descriptions of every card set that can't be squeezed into each monthly magazine price guide. One valuable benefit of the book is that card *back* photos are included. Often, it's hard to know the year and set of a card just by looking at its front.

Racing Die-Cast Collectibles, by Mark Zeske. $24.95 (Beckett Publications, 2000)

Large color pictures make this 256-page softcover a treat. The price-guide values from annual books like this may go out of date quickly. Glossy images of hard-to-find die-casts make this a tempting book for wishful hobbyists, though.

The NASCAR Way: The Business That Drives the Sport, by Robert G. Hagstrom (John Wiley and Sons, 1998)

How do drivers, team owners, and sponsors make money in NASCAR? How did Dale Earnhardt make millions from souvenir sales? The author supplies exciting, easy-to-understand answers to the money side of the sport/business.

Collectibles Makers

Action Performances Companies
Racing Collectibles Club of America
4707 East Baseline Road
Phoenix, AZ 85040
http://www.action-performance.com
http://www.goracing.com

American Racing Scene
19 Main Street
Scottsville, NY 14546
http://www.racingscene.com

Brookfield Collectors Guide
4707 East Baseline Road
Phoenix, AZ 85040

Darrell Gwynn Racing Collectibles
4850 SW 52nd Street
Davie, FL 33314

ERTL
P.O. Box 500, Department 776
Dyersville, IA 52040
http://www.racingchamps.com

The Franklin Mint
Franklin Center, PA 19091
http://www.franklinmint.com

Giovanni Plastics
337 Elm Street
Struthers, OH 44471
http://www.giovanniplastics.com

Hasbro Winners Circle
615 Elsinore Place
Cincinnati, OH 45202
http://www.hasbrocollectors.com
http://www.thewinnerscircle.com

Mattel Hot Wheels
333 Continental Boulevard
El Segundo, CA 90245
http://www.hotwheels.com

Playing Mantis
Johnny Lightning
3600 McGill Street, Suite 300
South Bend, IN 46628
http://www.playingmantis.com

Peachstate/GMP
37 Polite Road
Winder, GA 30680
http://www.peachgmop.com

Press Pass/Wheels
149 Gasoline Alley Drive
Mooresville, NC 28115

Racing Champions
800 Roosevelt Road, Building C, Suite 320
Glen Ellyn, IL 60137
http://www.racingchamps.com

Revell Collection
4707 East Baseline Road
Phoenix, AZ 85040
http://www.goracing.com

Revell-Monogram
8601 Waukegan
Morton Grove, IL 60053
http://www.revell-monogram.com

Sam Bass Illustration and Design
5725-B Concord Parkway South
Harrisburg, NC 28075
http://www.sambassart.com

Team Caliber
20901 Torrence Chapel Road, Suite 104
Cornelius, NC 28031
http://www.teamcaliber.com

Upper Deck
5905 Sea Otter Place
Carlsbad, CA 92008
http://www.upperdeck.com

White Rose Collectibles
P.O. Box 2701
York, PA 17405
http://www.whitrose.com

Museums

Many museums have ultimate collectibles on display: race-used NASCAR finery from uniforms to actual cars! Some museums represent various motorsports. This way, it's possible to see how stock car racing fits into the big picture of automobile history. Most museums try to reach collectors with gift shops. Check what items might be sold by mail.

Antique Auto & Race Car Museum
Stone City Mall, 3348 16th Street
Bedford, IN 47421
http://www.autoracemuseum.com

Birthplace of Speed Museum
160 E. Granada Boulevard
Ormond Beach, FL 32176

Daytona International Speedway and Visitors Center
1801 W. International Speedway Boulevard
Daytona Beach, FL 32114-1243

Dirt Motorsports Hall of Fame & Classic Car Museum
P.O. Box 240
Weedsport, NY 13166

Elliott Museum & Souvenir Center
P.O. Box 435
Dawsonville, GA 30534

Gilmore-CCCA Museum
6865 Hickory Road
Hickory Corners, MI 49060

Henry Ford Museum & Greenfield Village
P.O. Box 1970
Dearborn, MI 48121-1970

Himes Museum
15 O'Neil Avenue
Bayshore, NY 19706
http://www.geocities.com/MotorCity/Downs/6115

Indianapolis Motor Speedway Hall of Fame
4790 West 16th Street
Indianapolis, IN 46222

International Motorsports Hall of Fame
3198 Speedway Boulevard
Talladega, AL 35160

Joe Weatherly Museum
P.O. Box 500
Darlington, SC 29532

Motorsports Hall of Fame of America
43700 Expo Center Drive
Novi, MI 48375

National Auto Racing Hall of Fame Museum
P.O. Box 991
Flemington, NJ 08822

National Automobile Museum
10 Lake Street South
Reno, NV 89501

National Sprint Car Hall of Fame & Museum
One Sprint Capital Place
Knoxville, IA 50138

Richard Petty Museum
311 Branson Mill Road
Randleman, NC 27317

San Diego Automotive Museum
2080 Pan American Plaza #12
San Diego, CA 92101-1636

album: 1. a three-ring binder used to display cards kept in plastic sheets. 2. a paperback book for displaying collectible stickers.

assortment: a grouping of cards. The term implies that every card in the group is different. But there may be more than one of some cards unless the grouping has a label such as "100 *different*."

autograph: 1. something signed by the driver or race-team member shown. 2. a signed card of a race-team member, produced in limited quantity, certified as real by the manufacturer, and inserted in random packs.

Beckett: a registered trademark of Beckett Publications. The name of price-guide founder Dr. James Beckett is used often as a guideline for the value of a card. If a dealer will sell at "half Beckett," that means the card would cost half of the price listed in *Beckett Racing* magazine.

BGN: abbreviation for Busch Grand National. The Busch series of racing is considered a training ground for future Winston Cup drivers, although some drivers race in both circuits.

blankback: a card in which all the printing was omitted from the back. Often, a blankback was a printing mistake. Many collectors see blankbacks as incomplete cards with lesser value. See *wrongback*.

blister pack: a see-through, cardboard-backed package. Some of the product should be visible through the plastic fronts of blister packs.

book: short for *book value*, as from a price-guide book or magazine.

border: a framelike stripe surrounding the photo area on the card's front. For a card to be mint, all borders must be equal.

box: a vending container issued by card companies to be used by retailers. Usually containing 24 to 36 packs, it may contain a certain bonus card, sometimes printed on the bottom, as a reward for buying all the packs.

boxed set: cards sold in a complete set by the company. Often, boxed sets may be as few as 20 cards, containing only stars or rookies. Some boxed sets may be offered through only one store.

card stock: the paper or cardboard used to print the card. Card stock is judged by its thickness and color.

case: a sealed carton offered by a card company containing a specified number of factory-collated sets or boxes of card packs.

cello (SELL-o): an assortment of cards with wrapping that allows a buyer to see at least one card available in an assortment of cards. It is an older hobby term, referring to see-through cellophane wrapping.

centered: designating a card's image placed properly in the middle of the card. A card with an off-center photo is not considered mint.

checklist: 1. a complete listing of every card in a set. 2. a card that lists part of the cards in a set. Only unmarked checklists are considered mint.

collate: to put cards from a set in numerical order.

collectible: 1. a card or cards worthy of a collector's attention. 2. noncard items of memorabilia. 3. something worth money.

collector: one who collects motorsports cards first for fun, without seeking profit.

combination card (also called a *combo*): a card featuring more than one driver, car, or race-team member. Often, each of the racing personalities may not be noted by name on the card front. Photos showing pit action involving more than one race-team member are *not* combination cards.

commemorative: a card produced to highlight one event, such as winning one race.

common: one of the least-wanted cards in a set. The race-team member depicted is not popular or in demand, making the card affordable and easy to get.

condition: the look and health of a card.

convention: a large gathering of card dealers and collectors who buy, sell, and trade cards. A convention may last for several days, and is open to the public. Smaller gatherings are called *shows*.

convention issue: one or more items produced to promote one sports collectibles show. Often, the collectibles are only available at that show. Convention issues are sometimes sold or sometimes given away.

correction: a card issued by a manufacturer to correct an error on the card. The latter version may be more or less collectible, depending on its availability.

counterfeit: an illegally reprinted version of a card, which has no value but is wrongly sold as the actual card.

crease: a bend or fold that harms a card.

dealer: a person who buys, sells, or trades cards to make a profit. The dealer may also collect, but making money is the main goal.

decollate: to place cards in random order to be inserted into packages, a task often done by a machine.

die-cast: a miniature replica of a race car, made partially from die-cast steel.

die-cut: a card with part of its stock cut out, often to create fancy shapes.

display: retail items, such as posters or other advertisements, used in stores to help sell motorsports collectibles.

double-printed: a card that was issued in twice the quantity as other cards. When the company printed the sheet of cards, that card appeared one time more than the others.

driver: a racer; the person who drives the race car.

duplicate (also called a *dupe*): one of two identical collectibles.

error: a card with incorrect statistics, information, or photos on its front or back. Many errors go unfixed by the card companies, which may limit the card values.

extra: see *duplicate*.

factory-collated: designating a complete set, sorted by the manufacturer and sold as a unit.

food issue: a card or set made to help promote or sell certain food products.

franchise: a company that owns stores or restaurants of the same name in many towns. Burger King is an example of a franchise.

grade: to judge the condition of a card, looking at its creases, bent corners, and other possible problems.

graded: designating a card that has had its condition judged by a professional grading service. Services assign a score to the card, depending on its condition, such as 10.0 for a perfect card.

hand-sorted: designating a complete set of cards assembled by hand from numerous individual packages.

high numbers: the last series of a card set to be issued in packs. In the past, the last series was produced in lesser quantities and was harder to find.

hobby only: cards available only through hobby shops and card dealers.

hologram: 1. any of a number of specialized foil-like stickers and cards that give an image or photograph a three-dimensional appearance. 2. Upper Deck's diamond-shaped company trademark, placed on card backs to discourage counterfeiting.

hot pack: a pack in which every card is an insert or specialty card.

insert: 1. a card that is printed in limited quantities and randomly placed in only selected packs. Not considered part of a regular card set. 2. a noncard item, such as a poster or sticker, inserted one per pack to increase sales.

international issue: a card or set available in more than one country, not always published in English.

issue: 1. to make available. 2. one set or card from one source, such as a Press Pass issue.

laser-cut: cards designed and cut into unique shapes, often with pieces removed, all done by a laser.

lenticular: cards using a special hologram-like technology to make photos seem alive and three-dimensional.

limited edition: overused and misused, this term hints that cards from that set will be in short supply. In the past, companies would not tell if the edition was *limited* to thousands—or millions!

lot: an assortment of cards, related in some way, such as the same player, team, or set. The cards are sold as one unit.

mail-in cards: cards that can be obtained only from the company by mail. Often, mail-in cards require money and empty card wrappers.

manufacturer: a company that creates a product, for example, Upper Deck is a manufacturer of cards.

memorabilia: noncard items such as autographs, team publications, and equipment. See *collectible*.

miscut: a card improperly removed from the printing sheet. The card will have uneven centering and may be oddly shaped.

misprint: a card affected by poor printing, with a blurry photo, ink blot, or other untidy look.

multi-driver card: see *combination card*.

multi-sport: designating a set that features drivers and players from other sports.

National: short for National Sports Collector's Convention. This annual event is one of the nation's largest card shows, and is held in a different location each year.

odds: the chances of finding an insert card in a pack. Also called *ratio*.

off-center: a card with uneven borders.

oversized: designating cards bigger than the standard size of $2\frac{1}{2}$ by $3\frac{1}{2}$ inches (6.3 by 8.9 cm).

panel: two or more individual cards attached to one another, sometimes by a perforation.

parallel card: a card that is almost a twin of a regular card from a set, except for a special touch, such as embossed or die-cut features.

perforation: a dotted line, slightly cut, to show where cards can be separated or removed from a sheet. Dividing cards along perforated lines lessens their condition.

pitboard: colorful signs marking where each team is located on pit road at a race track. Cards have been made containing pieces of these.

plastic sheet: plastic or vinyl sheets with pockets to display and protect cards.

premium: 1. a special card or prize offered by mail from a company. 2. cards with more expensive special features, such as a thicker stock.

price guide: a book or magazine listing suggested cash values for cards. Prices rise and fall with time, so the date that a price guide was written is important.

promo: one or more collectibles made to promote a company, event, or future product release. Usually, promos are free samples or gifts (often cards) for people attending a collector's convention.

prototype: an early design for a card, which may differ from the future set. Sometimes, these cards are given as samples.

race-used: any equipment or clothing that was used during a race by teams or NASCAR officials.

random: not everywhere, such as "inserts can be found in random packs."

rare: an overused, often misused hobby term. A *rare* card is the hardest to find, harder to find than *scarce* cards.

redemption card: a card that, when mailed in, can be redeemed for special cards or prizes.

regional: cards distributed only in certain geographical regions. Regional card sets may focus on one team and be circulated only in the area near the team.

reprint: a later printing of an old card or die-cast, clearly marked as a *reprint*. Additionally, most reprints come with special markings to avoid confusion from originals.

retail only: available only through non-hobby stores, such as Kmart or Wal-Mart.

reverse: 1. the back of a card, showing statistics or biography. 2. a photo that has been printed backward because its negative is turned wrong-side-up during printing. Car numbers or writing will appear backward.

safety set (also known as a *police set*): a set with card backs having positive messages about obeying laws and behaving well. Sometimes, the cards are given away to kids one per week by police officers.

SASE: self-addressed, stamped envelope, sent to encourage a reply by mail.

scarce: see *rare*.

series: a set or a portion of a set. For instance, a four hundred card set may be issued in two stages, offering the first two hundred cards in the first series.

set: a collection of one of each card from one basic set, not including insert cards.

short-print: a card made in lesser quantities than others in the same set.

skip-numbered: not numbered in perfect sequence. Some card numbers may not exist because a driver was left out of the set following injury or contractual problems.

sleeve: a card-size plastic pouch used to protect and display one card.

standard-size card: one that is $2\frac{1}{2}$ by $3\frac{1}{2}$ inches (6.3 by 8.9 cm)

subset: a group of cards or die-casts, within a regular set, such as cards honoring one racing family or postseason award winners.

three-dimensional: cards with photographs that seem to move when tilted. Some three-dimensional cards may have images of more than one player.

tin: a decorative metal container or lid sold as a package containing one card or set.

uncut sheet: a sheet containing more than one card, left uncut by the manufacturer.

variation: a slightly different version of a card or die-cast. Variations usually occur when the company sees a mistake and tries to fix it. *Variation* refers to the error or the correction.

wax pack: an individually wrapped pack of cards. Previously, cards came in wrappers made of waxed paper.

WC: abbreviation for Winston Cup, the top level of NASCAR racing.

wrongback: a card with the back of another card from that set. A *wrongback* is more common than a *blankback*, but neither may see increased value.

ABOUT THE AUTHOR

Thomas S. Owens is the author of more than 50 books. His previous Millbrook Press titles include *Collecting Basketball Cards* and *Collecting Baseball Cards: The 21st Century Edition*. In addition to collecting, he enjoys gardening, walking, and playing with his two cats. Thomas lives in central Iowa with Diana Star Helmer, his author-illustrator wife.